CHALLENGE 2000

A Daily Meditation Program
Based on *The Spiritual Exercises*
of Saint Ignatius

Mark Link, S.J.

TABOR®
PUBLISHING
Allen, Texas

IMPRIMI POTEST
Bradley M. Schaeffer, S.J.

NIHIL OBSTAT
Rev. Glenn D. Gardner, J.C.D.
Censor Librorum

IMPRIMATUR
† Most Rev. Charles V. Grahmann
Bishop of Dallas

February 22, 1993

The Nihil Obstat and Imprimatur are official declarations
that the material reviewed is free of doctrinal or moral
error. No implication is contained therein that those
granting the Nihil Obstat and Imprimatur agree with the
contents, opinions, or statements expressed.

ACKNOWLEDGMENTS

Unless otherwise noted, Scripture quotations are from
Today's English Version text. Copyright © American
Bible Society 1966, 1971, 1976. Used by permission.

This book was originally published as the Challenge
Program. The content has been extensively revised and
reformatted for this volume.

Send all inquiries to:
Tabor Publishing
200 East Bethany Drive
Allen, Texas 75002-3804

Printed in Korea

ISBN 0-7829-0363-0

   2 3 4 5 6   98 97 96 95 94

VISION 2000

is a daily
meditation program.

The fourth book of the program,
Challenge 2000, is based on
The Spiritual Exercises of Saint Ignatius.

For other books in the program,
see page 10.

CONTENTS

Important Note

Challenge 2000 is a thirty-six-week program that divides into four parts:

I	Challenge	(twelve weeks)
II	Decision	(eleven weeks)
III	Journey	(six weeks)
IV	Victory	(seven weeks)

The ideal date to start the program is listed on the next page. It is ideal because beginning on this date "times" the program so that "Journey" (Jesus' suffering and death) starts Ash Wednesday Week and spans the Lenten Season (six weeks), and "Victory" (Jesus' suffering and death) starts Easter Week and spans the Easter Season (seven weeks).

To determine the ideal starting date, find the current year and read across. The date in the third column is the day the program will end in the *following* year, if the starting date is followed.

2

Year	Starting date	Ending date
1993	5 September	14 May
1994	18 September	27 May
1995	10 September	18 May
1996	1 September	10 May
1997	14 September	23 May
1998	6 September	15 May
1999	26 September	3 June
2000	17 September	26 May
2001	2 September	11 May
2002	22 September	31 May
2003	14 September	22 May
2004	29 August	7 May
2005	18 September	27 May
2006	10 September	19 May
2007	26 August	3 May
2008	14 September	23 May
2009	6 September	15 May

In some cases (for example, school use with faculty, staff, or students), it may be advisable to compromise the ideal starting date and shift it backward or forward, to allow the program to end before school ends.

About *Challenge 2000*

Master:	As the fish dies on the land, so you die in the midst of worldly business. To live again, the fish returns to water. You must return to solitude.
Disciple:	Must I therefore leave my business and go into a monastery?
Master:	Certainly not. Hold on to your business and go back to your heart.

ANTHONY DE MELLO, S.J.

Challenge 2000 is a daily meditation program that helps you hold on to your business and go back to your heart. It is based on *The Spiritual Exercises of Saint Ignatius.*

Normally, the Ignatian exercises are made in a retreat house, where retreatants work at them full time for thirty days. Saint Ignatius realized, however, that not everyone could take time to do this. So he developed a program for making the exercises at home over a longer period of time.

Like Saint Ignatius' program, *Challenge 2000* is divided into four parts:

Part I invites you to evaluate how well you are living your life according to the purpose for which God created you.

Part II invites you to know Jesus more intimately, follow him more lovingly, and serve him more ardently in building up God's Kingdom on earth.

Part III strengthens and confirms your decision to grow in knowledge, love, and service of Jesus.

Part IV begins your spiritual journey with Jesus in a life of love and service to God and neighbor.

There are three ways to use *Challenge 2000:*

- as part of a group that meets weekly;
- alone, under the direction of a spiritual guide;
- alone, without a guide or a group. If you do this, try to consult occasionally with a spiritual guide.

Daily Reflection Format

Each reflection exercise contains the same four elements:

- a Scripture passage,
- a story from life,
- an application to life,
- a concluding thought.

Begin each reflection by putting yourself in God's presence. One way to do this is to pray this prayer reverently:

Father, you created me
and put me on earth for a purpose.
Jesus, you died for me
and called me to complete your work.
Holy Spirit, you help me
to carry out the work
for which I was created and called.
In your presence and name—
Father, Son, and Spirit—
I begin my reflection.
May all my thoughts and inspirations
have their origin in you
and be directed to your glory.

The procedure for reflecting on the meditations is as follows:

- *Read* the reflection exercise slowly. When you finish, return to any phrase, sentence, or idea that struck you while reading.
- *Think* about the phrase, sentence, or idea that struck you. Might it be addressing something in your life?
- *Speak* to God about your thoughts as you would to a trusted friend.
- *Listen* for God's response. How might God answer you? Don't force this part of your reflection. Simply rest in God's presence with an open mind and heart.

N.B.: God often speaks to us outside the time of prayer. (Listening for God's response begins in prayer and continues subconsciously throughout the day.)

After each reflection, pray the Lord's Prayer slowly and record in a note pad some fruit (idea or thought) from your reflection.

N.B.: For handy reference, a summary of the "Daily Reflection Format" is printed on the inside front cover of this book.

Weekly Meeting Format

The purpose of the weekly meeting is for *support* and *sharing*. The agenda for each weekly meeting has three parts:

- the "Call to Prayer,"
- support and sharing,
- the "Call to Mission."

The leader calls each meeting to order promptly at the designated time. The "Call to Prayer" goes as follows:

A member lights a candle on the table around which the group is gathered. When the candle is lit, a second member reads aloud the following Bible passage and prayer:

> *[Jesus said,]*
> *"I am the light of the world. . . .*
> *Whoever follows me*
> *will have the light of life*
> *and will never walk in darkness."*
>
> JOHN 8:12

Lord Jesus, you said
that where two or three
come together in your name,
you are there with them.
The light of this candle
symbolizes your presence among us.

And, Lord Jesus,
where you are, there, too,
are the Father and the Spirit.

And so we begin our meeting
in the presence and the name
of the Father, the Son,
and the Holy Spirit.

The meeting proper begins with the leader responding briefly (two minutes) to these two questions.

- How faithful was I to my meditation commitment?
- Which meditation(s) did I find especially helpful—and why?

The leader then invites each member, in turn, to respond briefly (two minutes per person) to the same two questions. When all have responded, the leader opens the floor to anyone who wishes—

- to elaborate on his or her response to the second question, or
- to comment on another's response.

The leader ends the meeting promptly at the designated time with a "Call to Mission": a call to witness to Jesus and his teaching. A member prays as follows:

We conclude our meeting
by listening to Jesus say to us
what he said to his disciples
in his Sermon on the Mount:

"You are like light for the whole world.
A city built on a hill cannot be hid.
No one lights a lamp
and puts it under a bowl;
instead he puts it on a lampstand,
where it gives light
for everyone in the house.
In the same way
your light must shine before people,
so that they will see
the good things you do
and praise your Father in heaven."

MATTHEW 5:14-16

Then a member extinguishes the candle. The reader concludes:

The light of this candle
is now extinguished.
But the light of Christ in each of us
must continue to shine in our lives.
Toward this end we pray together
the Lord's Prayer: "Our Father . . ."

N.B.: For handy reference, the procedures for the "Call to Prayer" and the "Call to Mission" are printed on the last page and the inside back cover of this book.

10

I
CHALLENGE

The Spiritual Exercises of Saint Ignatius
is divided into four parts, called "weeks."
The "First Week," on which the first
twelve weeks of *Challenge 2000*
is based, focuses on this great mystery:
In spite of our sinfulness, the Trinity—
Father, Son, and Holy Spirit—loves us
beyond anything we can imagine.

This incredible truth inspires us to pray
with Saint Ignatius:

Lord,
teach me to be generous.
Teach me to serve you as you deserve;
to give and not to count the cost;
to fight and not to heed the wounds;
to toil and not to seek for rest;
to labor and not to ask for reward,
except to know
that I am doing your will.

11

1   Who is Ignatius?

Ignatius of Loyola founded the Society
of Jesus (Jesuits). It now numbers over
25,000 members in 112 countries. About
5,000 are in the United States, where,
among other ministries, they operate
nearly 30 universities and 50 high schools.

Perhaps Ignatius is best known for his
book *The Spiritual Exercises of Saint
Ignatius.* Actually, it is more a collection
of orderly notes than a book. And it is not
for a person "making" *The Spiritual
Exercises,* but for the director guiding the
person through them.

Ignatius was born in Spain just before the
discovery of America. His parents died
before he was sixteen, and he went to live
with a family friend.

Ignatius became skilled in horse riding
and in the use of the sword, the dagger,
and the crossbow. He had his share of
moral lapses. "Especially," wrote one of
his friends, "did he indulge in gambling,
dueling, and affairs with women."

Eventually, Ignatius became a soldier. During combat, his right leg was shattered by a cannonball. That event changed the course of his life.

This week's meditations pick up the story of Ignatius at this point. The grace you ask of God before beginning each daily meditation exercise is this:

Lord, may the life of Ignatius
inspire me to imitate him
in his search to find and serve you.

Weekly Instruction

Spend ten minutes on each meditation exercise. Follow the directions in the "Daily Reflection Format" on the inside cover of this book.

After each meditation, take a minute to review and to record (a few sentences) what went on in your mind and your heart during your reflection—some idea, thought, or feeling that stood out. Record your entries in a small notebook or pocket "Daily Organizer."

Now begin and God bless you.

WEEK 1
Day 1: Dreamer _____

*"You spoke to me, and . . .
your words filled my heart
with joy and happiness."*
JEREMIAH 15:16

The leg of Ignatius took nine months to
heal and left him with a lifelong limp.
While recuperating, he occupied his time
daydreaming and fantasizing. "At length
even he tired of self-induced fantasy
and called for romances and books
of chivalry, but the only two books to be
found in the house were a life of Christ
and a collection of saints' lives.
Slowly Ignatius conceived an admiration
for what he found there.
He still dreamed of glory,
but now it was to be God's glory.
He still ambitioned [serving a king] . . .
but the king was no longer
an earthly one."   THOMAS CLANCY,
"Ignatius Loyola: A Soldier-Saint?" *America* magazine

What turned my mind to spiritual things
and motivated me to undertake this
meditation program? What are some
feelings I have as I begin?

*God says to us:
With thy very wounds I will heal thee.*
THE TALMUD

[The father of the prodigal son said,]
"Let us celebrate with a feast! For this son
of mine was dead, but now he is alive;
he was lost, but now he has been found."

LUKE 15:23-24

After regaining his health, Ignatius went
to Montserrat. There he spent three days
writing out the sins of his life. Then he
confessed them to a priest.
"On the eve of the feast of Our Lady . . .
he went at night . . . to a poor man,
and stripping off his garments
he gave them to the poor man and
dressed himself in his desired clothing
and went to kneel before the altar
of Our Lady [staying the night there]. . . .
He left at daybreak. . . .
Crossing an old bridge on the Cardoner
River, he entered the town of Manresa.
There he spent the next ten months."

The Autobiography of Saint Ignatius of Loyola

Why should Ignatius write out his sins,
change clothes, keep an all-night vigil?

When I fall on my knees
with my face to the rising sun,
O Lord, have mercy on me.

NEGRO SPIRITUAL

WEEK 1
Day 3: Pray-er _____

*[Jesus] would go away to lonely places,
where he prayed.*

LUKE 5:16

The first months at Manresa were filled
with profound spiritual consolation.
Ignatius found lodging at a convent
operated by the Dominicans.
He begged his food, going door to door
with a tiny wooden bowl.
The kids in the town called after him,
" 'Here comes the man in the old sack.' " ...
Each day Inigo devoted seven hours
at Manresa to prayer. . . .
It was in these weeks that he discovered
what for the remainder of his life
was to prove his dearest book,
Imitation of Christ. . . .
But his chief delight
was to bury himself in prayer
in one of the thorn-choked caves
that opened along the Cardoner River."

LEONARD VON MATT and HUGO RAHNER,
Saint Ignatius of Loyola

How committed am I to seeking
and finding Jesus Christ?

*Turn to the Lord and pray . . .
now that [the Lord] is near.*

ISAIAH 55:6

WEEK 1
Day 4: Tortured Soul

*An angel from heaven
appeared to him and strengthened him.*

LUKE 22:43

Suddenly Ignatius' spiritual consolation
disappeared like the sun on a cloudy day.
His taste for spiritual things vanished as
suddenly as it had come. The whole idea
of conversion and turning his life over to
Jesus Christ seemed impossible. In an
effort to recapture the joy he once
experienced as he meditated on spiritual
things, Ignatius went on an eight-day fast.
It was all in vain! "He was on the brink
of desperation and suicide. Like a cry from
the very depths rose his appeal to the God
who deserted him: " 'Hasten, Lord, to
my aid, for I find no salvation in men and
creatures.' . . . God gave him answer.
Slowly there came into his tortured soul
the comfort of grace."

LEONARD VON MATT and HUGO RAHNER,
Saint Ignatius of Loyola

Can I recall a time when I had little or
no taste for spiritual things in my life?

*Never fear shadows. They simply mean
there's light shining somewhere nearby.*

RUTH RENKLE

WEEK 1
Day 5: Mystic _____

*He heard things
which cannot be put into words.*
2 CORINTHIANS 12:4

When peace returned to his tortured soul,
Ignatius began having mystical
experiences. Once as church bells pealed,
his soul soared skyward like an eagle, and
"in the imaged harmony of three organ
keys he contemplated the mystery of the
Trinity. Tears of joy ran down his
cheeks." On another occasion, at Mass,
he says he saw "how Jesus Christ was
there in the most holy sacrament." And
once, at prayer, "he saw with his inner
eyes the humanity of Christ." About these
experiences, he says in his autobiography
(in his usual third-person style), "The
things he saw . . . gave him such strength
in his faith, that he often thought to
himself: if there were no Bible to teach
these truths, he would be resolved to die
for them, only because of what he saw."

About what truths of my faith do I have
the kind of conviction that Ignatius had?

*All I have seen teaches me to trust
the Creator for all I have not seen.*
RALPH WALDO EMERSON

WEEK 1
_____ Day 6: Transformed Person

[Jesus said,]
"How fortunate you are to see the things
you see! I tell you that many
prophets and kings wanted to see
what you see, but they could not, and
to hear what you hear, but they did not."

LUKE 10:23-24

One September afternoon Ignatius was
walking along the Cardoner. Suddenly
God gave him a "brilliant enlightenment"
of "faith and theology"
and of the "spiritual life."
Later, he wrote
that all the enlightenments of his life
combined "would not, in his judgment,
be as great as what he experienced
on that occasion."
It was as though he were transformed
into another person.
"He threw himself down on his knees
before a crucifix which stood nearby
to express his gratitude to God."

The Autobiography of Saint Ignatius of Loyola

At what point in my life was my faith
strongest? How do I account for this?

Give me faith, Lord,
and let me help others find it.

LEO TOLSTOY

WEEK 1
Day 7: Spiritual Guide _____

*Jesus said to [Simon and Andrew],
"Come with me. . . ."
They left their nets and went with him.*

MARK 1:17-18

Ignatius was overwhelmed by his
enlightenment. He saw clearly how the
risen Jesus and God's Kingdom are present
among us, right now. He also saw clearly
how the struggle between good and evil
is going on in every heart, right now.
More importantly, he saw how to
communicate to others the realization
that he had received concerning Jesus and
God's Kingdom. And so he wrote what is
now called *The Spiritual Exercises of Saint
Ignatius*. It is upon these meditation
exercises that *Challenge 2000* is based.

If Jesus offered to give me any grace
I wanted as I start *Challenge 2000*,
what grace would I ask for?
Why this?

*Lord, teach me to be generous.
Teach me to serve you as you deserve;
to give and not to count the cost . . .
to labor and not to ask for reward,
except to know that I am doing your will.*

SAINT IGNATIUS, "Prayer for Generosity"

WEEKLY MEETING
_____ Sharing Agenda

The following questions are based on this week's daily meditations. They are intended to facilitate sharing. Simply pick out one or two questions you would feel comfortable sharing and respond to them.

1 What motivated me to embark upon this meditation program? What is one question in my mind as I begin?

2 Why should Ignatius write out his sins, exchange clothes, keep an all-night vigil?

3 How committed am I to discovering and following Jesus?

4 Can I recall a time when I had little or no taste for spiritual things?

5 What truths of faith do I find hard to accept? A little difficult to accept?

6 At what time in my life was my faith strongest? How do I account for this?

7 If I could ask for one grace as I start _Challenge 2000,_ what would I ask for?

2 Who am I?

Someone said, "I am three persons: the
person I think I am, the person you think
I am, and the person I *really* am."

The daily meditations of this week are
designed to help you get a clearer picture
of the *real* you—not the "you"
you think you are, not the "you" other
people think you are, but the "you" you
really are.

The grace you ask of God before each
meditation is this:

*Lord, give me eyes to see myself
as I really am.*

Weekly Instruction

The meditation procedure for this and all
subsequent weeks remains the same. It
is as follows:

Reflect on one meditation each day. Spend
ten minutes on it, following the directions
in the "Daily Reflection Format" on the
inside front cover of this book.

After each meditation, take a minute to
review and to record (a few sentences)
what went on in your mind and your heart

during your reflection—the idea, thought, or feeling that stood out. Record your entries in a small notebook or a pocket "Daily Organizer."

The disposition to have as you begin *Challenge 2000* is one of generosity. Remember that for each step you take toward God, God will take a dozen steps toward you.

Daily Reading

The daily Bible readings listed below are merely suggestions. Feel free to read them or not, as the Spirit moves you.

If you read them, read only the chapter and verses indicated. Pause briefly before each reading to remind yourself that you are about to read God's word. Likewise, pause after each reading to let that word sink into your heart as rain sinks into dry soil.

1 Lord, who are we   Ps 8
2 We bear your image   Gen 1:26-31
3 You care about us   Mt 10:26-31
4 You are our God   Rev 21:1-4
5 You see our heart   Gal 6:7-10
6 You make us new   2 Cor 5:16-19
7 We are your children   1 Jn 3:1-3

WEEK 2
Day 1 _____

*O LORD . . . what are human beings
that you are mindful of them,
mortals that you care for them? . . .
You have made them
a little lower than God,
and crowned them with glory and honor.*

PSALM 8:1, 4-5 (NRSV)

Philosopher Arthur Schopenhauer was
walking down the street one day. He was
lost in thought. Quite accidentally he
bumped into another pedestrian. Still lost
in thought, he kept on walking.
The pedestrian shouted, "Well, who do
you think you are?" The absent-minded
philosopher was heard to mumble,
"Who am I? How I wish I knew!"
Astronaut John Glenn says a standard
test for astronaut candidates was to have
them give twenty answers to the question
"Who am I?" "The first few answers,"
he said, "were easy. After that,
it got harder."

What are three significant answers
I would give to the question "Who am I?"

*A humble knowledge of myself
is a surer way to God
than a search after learning.*

THOMAS A KEMPIS

Then God said,
"And now we will make human beings;
they will be like us and resemble us."

GENESIS 1:26

Cartoonist Thomas Nast was at a party
with some close friends. Someone asked
him to draw a quick caricature of each
person present. He obliged. Then he
passed the sketches around for everyone
to look at. There was a lot of laughing and
joking. Then something unexpected became
evident. While everyone recognized the
others instantly, few recognized themselves
at first glance. When it comes to ourselves,
we often have a blind spot. That is, we
fail to see ourselves as others see us. We
fail to recognize our most obvious traits:
our strengths, weaknesses, mannerisms.

What two words would I pick
to describe myself? What two words
might my best friend pick to describe me?
What two words might God pick
to describe me?
How would I account for the differences?

If I saw myself
as my friends and other people see me,
I would need an introduction.

AUTHOR UNKNOWN

WEEK 2
Day 3 _____

*[Jesus said,] "Even the hairs
of your head have all been counted."*

LUKE 12:7

They say the heads of blonds contain
about 150,000 hairs; brunets, about 125,000;
and redheads about 100,000. It's hard to
verify this count. But the big numbers
help us appreciate the example Jesus used
one day. Pointing to a flock of sparrows,
he said to the people, "Aren't five sparrows
sold for two pennies? Yet not one sparrow
is forgotten by God." No doubt Jesus ran
his fingers through the hair of a little girl,
smiled, and said,
"Even the hairs of your head
have all been counted.
So do not be afraid; you are worth
much more than many sparrows!"
In other words, Jesus assures us that we
are precious in God's sight. God treasures
us beyond our wildest imagining. Thus,
one answer to the question "Who am I?"
is this: "I am someone treasured by God."

Why does God treasure me?

*Under all the false, overloaded,
glittering masquerade,
there is in every person a noble nature.*

B. AUERBACH

They said to one another,
"Here comes that dreamer. . . .
Let's kill him. . . . Then we will see
what becomes of his dreams."

GENESIS 37:19-20

It was a summer day in Washington when
Martin Luther King, Jr., spoke these
memorable words to a huge crowd:
"I have a dream that one day this nation
will rise up and live out the true meaning
of its creed: 'We hold these truths to be
self-evident; that all men are created
equal.' I have a dream that one day on the
red hills of Georgia the sons of former
slaves and the sons of former slaveowners
will be able to sit down together at the
table of brotherhood. . . . This is our hope.
This is the faith that I go back to the
South with. With this faith, we will be
able to hew out of the mountain of despair
a stone of hope."

What is a dream I have
for our nation as a whole?
For myself as an individual?

It isn't a calamity
to die with dreams unfulfilled,
but it is a calamity not to dream.

BENJAMIN E. MAYS

WEEK 2
Day 5 _____

Each one should judge his own conduct . . .
without having to compare it
with what someone else has done.

GALATIANS 6:4

A woman was riding on a train. Suddenly
she caught sight of a white cottage on a
hillside. Against the backdrop of dark
green grass, the cottage sparkled in the
sun and was a lovely sight. Months later
the same woman was on the same train.
Now it was winter, and snow covered the
ground. The woman remembered the
cottage and watched for it. This time she
was shocked. Against the backdrop of the
sparkling snow, the cottage looked dirty
and drab. There's a lesson here. We tend
to compare ourselves with those around
us. The story of the cottage shows how
misleading this can be. It all depends on
who happens to be around us when we
make our judgment.

What criterion should I use
to judge how well I am doing?

In the twilight of life,
God will not judge us on our earthly
possessions and human successes,
but on how well we have loved.

SAINT JOHN OF THE CROSS

The LORD said . . .
"[People look] at the outward appearance,
but I look at the heart."

1 SAMUEL 16:7

The movie *Mask* is based on the true story
of sixteen-year-old Rocky Dennis. A rare
disease made the bones of his face grow
larger than they should. As a result,
Rocky's face was horribly misshapen. He
never pitied himself or gave way to anger.
Instead, he accepted his appearance as it
was. One day Rocky and some friends
were at an amusement park. They went
into a "house of mirrors" and began to
laugh at how distorted their bodies and
faces looked. Suddenly Rocky saw
something that startled him. One mirror
distorted his misshapen face in a way that
made it appear normal. In that mirror
Rocky was strikingly handsome. For the
first time, Rocky's friends saw him as he
was on the inside: a beautiful person.

What do I like best about my "inside"
person? My "outside" person?

It is better to be patient than powerful.
It is better to win control over yourself
than over whole cities.

PROVERBS 16:32

WEEK 2
Day 7 _____

*We know that when Christ appears,
we shall be like him.*

1 JOHN 3:2

There's a legend about an Indian boy who
found an eagle's egg. He took the egg
home and put it in a chicken's nest. A
baby eagle hatched out of the egg and grew
up with the other baby chickens. The little
eagle thought he was a chicken and did
what the other chickens did. He scratched
in the dirt, made chicken noises, and
thrashed his wings about awkwardly,
rising only a few feet off the ground. One
day the little eagle saw a beautiful bird
soaring high in the sky above him. It
glided on the wind in great circles. "What
a marvelous bird!" the eagle said to an
adult chicken standing nearby. "That's
an eagle," said the adult chicken. "It's the
king of the birds. But don't get any silly
ideas. You could never be like him or do
what he's doing."

How is this story a parable of Jesus,
myself, and who I really am?

*We are stardust, we are golden—
and we've got to get ourselves
back to the garden.*

JONI MITCHELL

WEEKLY MEETING
Sharing Agenda

_____

The following questions are based on this week's daily meditations. They are intended to facilitate sharing. Simply pick out one or two questions you would feel comfortable sharing and respond to them.

1 What is the most revealing or insightful response I could make to the question "Who am I?"

2 What two words best describe me? Why these?

3 What is one talent I have? How am I using it? How might I put it to better use in the future?

4 What is one dream I have, and what is one thing I am doing to try to realize it?

5 What criterion do I use to judge how well I am doing as a person? Using this criterion, how would I rate myself on a scale of one (low) to seven (high)?

6 What is one fact about my "inside self" that very few people, even close friends, are not aware of?

7 How is the legend of the eagle a parable of who I really am? What might I learn from the parable?

3 Do I rejoice in who I am?

Two women named Hooker wrote letters to columnist Ann Landers. The first woman resented her name. The second rejoiced in it.

The second woman explained that a sense of humor has made all the difference. For example, she said that when she gets crude phone calls asking how much she charges, she answers, "More than you can afford, Buddy!" She added, "Believe it or not, there are advantages to being a Hooker. Your name is rarely misspelled, and no one ever forgets it."

The reaction of the two women is typical of how different people react differently to the same situation.

This week's meditations invite you to ask, What is my reaction to who I am? How happy am I with myself: my looks, my talent, and so forth? The grace you ask of God before each daily meditation is:

God, give me
the serenity to accept—even joyfully—
that part of myself that I can't change,
the courage to change that part of myself
that I ought to change, and
the wisdom to know one from the other.

SERENITY PRAYER (adapted)

Weekly Instruction

After each meditation, be sure to continue the practice of reviewing and recording the thought, idea, or feeling that struck you most during your prayer.

The value of keeping a record of each meditation cannot be overestimated. You might address your words directly to God. For example, you might write:

"Lord, thank you for helping me see more clearly than ever that 'what I am' is your gift to me and 'what I become' is my gift back to you."

Daily Reading

Again, the Bible readings are optional. If you read them, read only the chapter and verses indicated. Pause briefly before each reading to remind yourself that you are about to read God's word. Pause after each reading to let it sink into your heart.

1 Lord, you know me   Ps 139:1-6
2 My grace is sufficient   2 Cor 12:7-10
3 Take up your cross   Mt 16:21-25
4 Run to win   Phil 3:12-16
5 Blessings in disguise   2 Pt 1:3-9
6 Parable of the sower   Lk 8:5-8
7 Meaning of the parable   Lk 8:11-15

34

WEEK 3
Day 1 _____

[Lord,]
when my bones were being formed,
carefully put together
in my mother's womb, . . .
you knew that I was there—
you saw me before I was born.

PSALM 139:15-16

A teacher gave this assignment to her
students: "Find an unnoticed flower around
your home and study it. Note its petals—
their shape and their color. Turn it over
and look at its underside. As you do,
remember this is your flower. It might
have died unappreciated had you not
found it and admired it." Next day, after
the students reported on their flowers, the
teacher said: "Each one of us is like your
flower. We are unique. But we often go
unappreciated because no one takes the
time to notice our unique beauty. Each of
us is a masterpiece of God. There won't
be another person like us—ever again."

What is one special gift or unique talent
that God has blessed me with?

Lord, help me to root out from my heart
everything that is of my own planting
and to restore to my heart
everything that is of your planting.

*I have the strength to face all conditions
by the power that Christ gives me.*

PHILIPPIANS 4:13

Tom Dempsey was born with no right
hand and with only half a right foot. But
that didn't stop him from playing football
in junior college. He got so good as a place
kicker that the New Orleans Saints signed
him. On November 8, 1970, the Saints
were trailing Detroit 17–16 with two
seconds to go on Detroit's forty-five-yard
line. The Saints' coach turned to Tom and
said, "Go out and give it your best shot!"
When the holder set the ball down, it was
exactly sixty-three yards from the uprights.
The rest is history. Tom broke the NFL
field goal record by seven yards. Later he
told *Newsweek* magazine, "I couldn't follow
the ball that far. But I saw the official's
arms go up and I can't describe how great
I felt."

What is the closest thing to a "handicap"
that God has given me?
How might I turn it into an "advantage"?

*I thank God for my handicaps,
for through them, I have found
myself, my work, and my God.*

HELEN KELLER

WEEK 3
Day 3

[Jesus said,] "If anyone wants to come with me . . . he must forget himself, carry his cross, and follow me."

MARK 8:34

James Du Pont recalls this childhood episode. He awoke one night to hear his mother sobbing loudly. It was the first time he had ever heard her cry. Then he heard his father speaking to her. James says: "My dad's voice was low and troubled as he tried to comfort mother; and in their anguish they both forgot about the nearness of my bedroom." Describing the impact this experience had on him, James says: "While their problem . . . has long since been solved and forgotten, the big discovery I made that night is still with me. Life is not all hearts and flowers. It's hard and cruel . . . much of the time."

When did I learn firsthand that life can be hard and cruel? What can I do to make sure that life's hardships and cruelty will make me better—and not bitter?

Things "turn out best"
for the people who make the best
of the way things "turn out."
ART LINKLETTER

[Jesus said,]
"Knock, and the door will be opened."
MATTHEW 7:7

When Glenn Cunningham was seven
years old, his legs were burned so badly
that doctors considered amputation. At
the last minute they decided against it.
One doctor patted Glenn's shoulder and
said, "When the weather turns warm,
we'll get you into a chair on the porch."
Glenn replied, "I don't want to sit. I want
to walk and run, and I will." Two years
later Glenn was running. He wasn't
running fast, but he was running. When
Glenn went to college, his extracurricular
activity was track. Now he was running
not to prove the doctors wrong but
because he was good at it. Then came the
Berlin Olympics. Glenn not only qualified
but also broke the Olympic record for the
1,500-meter race. The boy who wasn't
supposed to walk again became the world's
fastest human.

How tenaciously am I willing to strive—
against odds—to reach a goal I value?

Big shots
are only little shots who keep shooting.
CHRISTOPHER MORLEY

WEEK 3
Day 5 _____

Be glad about . . . [the] trials you suffer.
Their purpose is to prove that your faith
is genuine. Even gold . . . is tested
by fire; and so your faith . . . must also
be tested, so that it may endure.

1 PETER 1:6-7

Near Cripple Creek in Colorado, telluride
ore contains gold and tellurium. Early
refining methods couldn't separate the
two, so the ore was thrown away. One day
a miner mistook a lump of ore for coal and
tossed it into his stove. Later he found
beads of pure gold littering the ashes of
his stove. The heat had burned away the
tellurium, leaving the gold in a purified
state. We are like telluride ore. Gold is
inside us, but it often takes a "fiery trial"
in the "stove of affliction" to bring it out
of us.

What trial or affliction in my life helped
me most to discover the gold inside me?

It ain't possible to explain some things.
It's interesting to wonder on them and
do some speculation, but the main thing is
you have to accept it—
take it for what it is
and get on with your growing.

JIM DODGE

"Happy are you poor;
the Kingdom of God is yours!"
LUKE 6:20

Critics call Marc Chagall the greatest
artist of the twentieth century. In *My Life,*
Chagall tells how he grew up in a poor
Jewish family in Russia. His interest in
art was aroused when he watched a
classmate copy a picture from a magazine.
Shortly afterward, when his mother was
baking bread, he touched her flour-
smeared elbow and said, "Mama, I want
to be an artist." Chagall's dream took him
to Paris, where he won worldwide acclaim.
He never forgot his poverty; he rejoiced
in it and felt that it helped him, saying:
"The very worst thing to have too early
is a little success, a little money . . . a little
satisfaction. The little satisfactions . . .
hold you back from big dedication."

What experience from my childhood
or early family life
is impacting my present life
in a major way—for good?

Happy are they who grieve not
for what they have not,
but give thanks for what they do have.
AUTHOR UNKNOWN

WEEK 3
Day 7 _____

*"Once there was a man
who went out to sow grain."*
MARK 4:3

A saying reads, "I will set my face to the
wind and scatter my seeds on high."
That's a poetic way of saying that God
expects us to use our talents (seeds) to
better our world. It also warns us that
we will meet difficulties (wind) doing this.
Consider an example. Before dying,
someone wrote: "We have to believe every
part of our lives has value. What has value
can be shared. I've something to share:
Embrace every situation with confidence
in its meaning and value! I think that's
what Jesus meant when he called us the
light of the world. He wants us to believe
in our meaning and value. To believe in
him and his Father, we have to believe in
ourselves."

What tends to keep me from believing
that my life has meaning and value?
How can I overcome this stumbling block?

*Each is given a bag of tools,
A shapeless mass, / A book of rules;
And each must make— / Ere life is flown—
A stumbling block / Or a steppingstone.*
R. L. SHARPE

WEEKLY MEETING
Sharing Agenda

The following questions are based on this week's daily meditations. They are intended to facilitate sharing. Simply pick out one or two questions you would feel comfortable sharing and respond to them.

1 What do I consider to be one of God's best gifts to me?

2 What do I consider to be one cross that God has given me? How might I turn it into a blessing?

3 Can I recall a time in my life when I felt that life can be hard, cruel, or unfair?

4 How tenacious am I in striving for a goal I really value? Example?

5 What trial or affliction in my life helped me unearth the gold in my life that I didn't realize I had?

6 What aspect of my early family life is impacting my present life—for good? Example?

7 How meaningful or valuable do I consider my current life to be? Why?

4   How meaningful is my life?

Jerry Kramer played for the Green Bay
Packers and made the All-Pro team four
times. During his career he kept a diary.
Later it was published under the title of
*Instant Replay: The Green Bay Diary of
Jerry Kramer*.

In one entry, Jerry talks about the movie
Cool Hand Luke. Luke was a wild character
who was in and out of prison all of his life.
The last time he got out of prison, he
went into a church, knelt down, and said
something like this:
"Old Man, whadaya got planned for me?
What's next? Whadaya put me on earth
for?" Commenting on the scene, Kramer
writes:

"I ask myself the same questions. I often
wonder where my life is heading, and
what's my purpose here on earth besides
playing the silly games I play every
Sunday. I feel there's got to be more to life
than that. There's got to be some reason
for it. . . . I didn't come up with any
answers this morning. I just thought
about it for a while."

This week's meditations focus on the meaning of life. The grace you ask for is:

Lord, help me discover the meaning that you intended my life to have when you created me.

Weekly Instruction

Consider making a shortened version of the Scripture passage that introduces each meditation. For example, you might shorten the Scripture introduction for the first day of this week to read:

"Where from? Where to?"

Make an effort to recall it occasionally during the day. You might even write it on a slip of paper and place it on your desk as a reminder.

Daily Reading

1	I chose you	Jer 1:4–8
2	Your life is short	Ps 90:1–6
3	Are you seeing	Mt 13:14–16
4	Find the Kingdom	Lk 12:29–34
5	Choose the Kingdom	Mk 8:36–38
6	Who/what to fear	Lk 12:4–5
7	Faith is not enough	Jas 2:14–17

WEEK 4
Day 1 _____

*"Where have you come from
and where are you going?"*
GENESIS 16:8

King Edwin lived in seventh-century
England. One day he was talking to a close
friend about the shortness of life. His
friend made this comparison: "O king,
recall the room where you meet with your
officers on cold winter nights in front of
the huge fireplace. During those meetings,
a lone sparrow sometimes flies into the
room through an opening, exiting just as
quickly through another opening. Life is
like the swift flight of that sparrow. While
it is inside the room, safe from the cold,
it enjoys a brief space of fair weather. But
then it vanishes again into the night. No
one knows whence it came or where it
goes. So it is with us, O king. Our time
on earth is brief, like the flight of that
sparrow. No one knows whence we came
or where we go."

If someone asked me
where I came from and
where I am going, what would I say?

*Make sure the thing you're living for
is worth dying for.*
CHARLES MAYES

Teach us how short our life is,
so that we may become wise.

PSALM 90:12

In the play *Our Town*, Emily dies giving
birth to her first child. She learns from
the dead that it is possible for her to
choose one day from her life and relive it.
But they all advise against it. Emily
ignores their advice and chooses to relive
one of the happiest days of her life, her
twelfth birthday. She begins. But before
she gets halfway through the day, she
cries out, "I can't. I can't go on. . . . We
don't have time to look at one another.
Take me back up the hill to my grave."
Later she asks one of the dead, "Do
humans ever realize life while they live
it?" The dead person pauses a minute and
says sadly, "No. The saints and poets,
maybe—they do some."

To what extent do I tend to live
in the fast lane, forgetting to stop and
smell the flowers now and then?

Our lives are songs; God writes the words
And we set them to music at pleasure;
And the song grows glad, or sweet or sad,
As we choose to fashion the measure.

ELLA WHEELER WILCOX

*[Jesus said,] "They look, but do not see,
and they listen, but do not hear."*

MATTHEW 13:13

Starbuck is a character in the play *The Rainmaker*. He's unhappy with life but doesn't know why. Another character, named Lizzie, says it's his own fault. He never pauses long enough to see life as it really is. Then Lizzie gives him an example. She says that sometimes she watches her father playing cards with her brothers. At first she sees only a man, not very attractive or interesting to look at. But as she continues to look, she begins to see other things. "I'll see little things I never saw in him before. Good things and bad things—queer little habits I never . . . paid any mind to. And suddenly I know who he is and I love him so much I could cry! And I want to thank God I took the time to see him real."

What one thing, especially, keeps me from pausing to see life and people as they really are?

*Nothing here below is profane
for those who know how to see.
On the contrary, everything is sacred.*

TEILHARD DE CHARDIN

[Jesus said,] "Don't be all upset . . .
about what you will eat and drink. . . .
Your Father knows
that you need these things.
Instead, be concerned with his Kingdom,
and he will provide you with these things."

LUKE 12:29-31

A motorist drove into a "full-service"
station. Three attendants charged out to
service his car. When they finished, the
motorist paid for the ten gallons of gas
and drove off. Three minutes later he
returned, saying, "I'm embarrassed to ask
you this, but did anyone put gas in my
car?" The attendants looked at one another.
In their rush to serve, they had forgotten
the gas. What happened to the attendants
sometimes happens to us. We get so
involved in living life that we forget why
God gave us life.

In what sense might I be like
the attendants at the gas station?

While it is well enough
to leave footprints on the sands of time,
it is even more important
to make sure they point
in a commendable direction.

JAMES BRANCH CABELL

WEEK 4
Day 5 _____

[Jesus said,]
"Whoever loses his life for me
and for the gospel will save it."

MARK 8:35

There's a movie star in John O'Hara's
novel *The Last Laugh*. He has been an
SOB all of his life. Eventually his career
goes into a tailspin, and he ends up a
complete zero. Realizing his situation, he
says to himself, "At least I was once the
idol of movie fans all over the country.
Nobody can take that away from me."
When you read this, you feel like laughing
out loud and saying, "Big deal, buster!
Who cares now!"

If my life continues on its current course,
how content will I be at death?

To every man there openeth
A way and ways and a way.
And the high soul climbs the high way,
And the low soul gropes the low,
And in between, on the misty flats,
The rest drift to and fro.
But to every man there openeth
A high way and a low.
And every man decideth
The way his soul shall go.

JOHN OXENHAM

[Jesus said,]
"Does a person gain anything
if he wins the whole world
but loses his life?"

MARK 8:36

A basketball team had just celebrated a prayer service before playing in the state tournament. During the service, the chaplain said to the team, "The important thing ten years from now won't be whether or not you won the state championship. Rather, it will be what you became in the process of trying to win it." After the prayer service, the coach said to the players: "Sit down a minute. Our chaplain said something that is bothering me. I wonder what we've become trying to put together a winning season. Have we become more loyal to one another? More loving? Better Christians? I hope to God that we have. Because if we haven't, we've failed God, we've failed one another, we've failed ourselves."

How would I answer the coach's question regarding my life up to this point?

You can't turn back the clock.
But you can wind it up again.
BONNIE PRUDDEN

WEEK 4
Day 7 _____

*"I am now giving you the choice
between life and death . . .
and I call heaven and earth
to witness the choice you make."*
DEUTERONOMY 30:19

On the night of April 15, 1912, the *Titanic*
hit an iceberg and sank, taking over 1,500
lives. Seventy years later a magazine
advertisement cited the disaster and asked
its readers: "If you'd been on the *Titanic*
when it was sinking, would you have
rearranged the deck chairs?" At first we
say to ourselves, "That's a silly question."
But then we get the point the ad is
making. Our world is facing a spiritual
disaster, and many of us are "rearranging
the deck chairs."

The advertisement invites me to ask, Am
I so caught up in my own little world that
I am forgetting about the larger world?
Am I so concerned about my own little
world that I am forgetting that God
created me and placed me in the larger
world for a purpose?

*A time like this demands
Strong minds, great hearts,
true faith, and ready hands!*
JOSIAH G. HOLLAND

1 If someone asked me where I came from and where I am going, what would I say? How well would my present life reflect my answer?

2 When was the last time I stopped to smell the flowers? Why did I stop to do it then?

3 What is one thing, especially, that keeps me from stopping to smell the flowers? How valid is this reason?

4 To what extent am I so involved in living that I am missing the point of why God gave me life?

5 Assuming my life continues in the direction it is currently going, how successful in God's eyes will it have been?

6 Where am I putting my priorities: on "becoming" or "acquiring"? What is some concrete evidence of this?

7 To what extent might I be rearranging the deck chairs on a ship that is sinking?

5   How real is God for me?

The film *Laura* is about a young detective
assigned to investigate the murder of a
young woman name Laura. One night
someone came to her apartment and fired
a shotgun blast into her face. For the next
week the detective spends all of his time
in Laura's apartment, checking
everything—even reading her diary for a
clue that might lead to her killer.

Then something strange happens. The
more the detective learns about Laura, the
more he finds himself becoming emotionally
involved. He finds himself falling in love
with her. One night, as he ponders her
case in her apartment, the key turns in
the lock. The door opens, and there stands
Laura.

To make a long story short, the slain
woman was someone who had used Laura's
apartment while Laura was away on
vacation. The movie ends with Laura and
the detective falling in love, marrying, and
living happily ever after.

The movie is a kind of modern parable of
what God wants to happen to each of us.
God wants us to study the world, fall in
love with its Creator, and live happily
forever after.

This week's meditations seek to help you do just that. The grace you ask for is:

Lord my God, teach my heart where and how to seek you, where and how to find you.
ANSELM OF CANTERBURY

Weekly Instruction

Before each meditation this week, make a special effort to place yourself in God's presence. As you do, keep in mind that trying to *feel* God's presence is almost always wrong. A *sensible* awareness of God's presence is a gift. You cannot make it happen. All you can do is open yourself to receive the gift.

Daily Readings

1 Always there   Ps 46
2 Come no closer   Gen 3:1-6
3 I will be with you   Gen 28:10-17
4 In a whisper   1 Kgs 19:11-13
5 Only God knows   2 Cor 12:1-12
6 I long for you   Ps 42
7 You know me   Ps 139:1-6

WEEK 5
Day 1 _____

God is our shelter and strength,
always ready to help in times of trouble.

PSALM 46:1

In *Today's Christian Woman*, Sharon
O'Donohue writes that in working with
young people, she suddenly realized that
she herself had been spared a lot of grief
as a teenager. When she probed for a
reason, she came up with this answer:
"In the early stages of my childhood,
I had been taught that someone
by the name of God . . .
was always present. . . .
How did I know? Because I had a patient
mom who listened to all my questions,
who used everyday situations to teach me
that God was always there."

What role did the faith
of my parents or guardians play
in building my own personal faith,
especially my faith
in God and God's personal care for me?

God be in my eyes—and in my looking;
God be in my mouth—and in my speaking;
God be in my mind—and in my knowing;
God be in my heart—and in my loving;
God be in all my life—and all my living.

ANONYMOUS

God said . . .
"Take off your sandals,
because you are standing on holy ground."

EXODUS 3:5

In *The Golden String,* Bede Griffiths
describes a childhood experience. He was
walking outside one summer evening and
suddenly became aware of how beautifully
the birds were singing. He wondered why
he had never heard them sing like this
before. Continuing to walk, he came to a
field. Everything was quiet and still.
As he stood there, watching the sun slip
below the horizon, he felt inclined to kneel
down. It was as though God were there
in a tangible way. He wrote later,
"Now that I look back on it, it seems to
me it was one of the decisive moments of
my life."

Can I recall a childhood experience
that had a powerful effect on my life?
When? What?

Earth's crammed with heaven,
And every common bush aflame with God;
And only he who sees takes off his shoes—
The rest sit round it
and pluck blackberries.

E. B. BROWNING

WEEK 5
Day 3 _____

*"I am the LORD. . . . I will be with you
and protect you wherever you go."*
GENESIS 28:13, 15

Thor Heyerdahl won fame by navigating
a small raft, called *Kon Tiki,* across 4,300
miles of ocean. Oddly enough, Thor once
had a deathly fear of water. He overcame
it when a canoe carrying him capsized
near a waterfall in a Canadian river.
As the rapids swept him toward the falls,
a strange thought came into his mind.
He would soon learn which of his parents
was right. His father believed in God; his
mother did not. Then something strange
happened. The Lord's Prayer flashed into
his mind, and he began to pray. A burst
of energy shot through him. He began to
battle the rapids. Some unseen power was
helping him. A few minutes later he made
it to shore. That day Thor lost his fear of
water and gained the sure knowledge that
his father was right.

Can I recall a time when God seemed to
help me in a special way? When? How?

*God's presence is not discerned
at the time when it is upon us,
but afterwards when we look back.*
JOHN HENRY NEWMAN

"I am the LORD your God; . . .
'Do not be afraid; I will help you.' "
ISAIAH 41:13

One night Dr. Martin Luther King, Jr.,
was just about to doze off when the phone
rang. A voice on the other end said,
"Listen, nigger, we've taken all we want
from you. Before next week, you'll be
sorry you ever came to Montgomery."
Dr. King hung up. Suddenly all his fears
came crashing down on him. He got up
and heated a pot of coffee. Then he sat
down at the kitchen table, bowed his head,
and prayed: "People are looking to me for
leadership, and if I stand before them
without strength and courage, they too
will falter. I am at the end of my powers.
I have nothing left. I've come to the point
where I can't face it alone." At that
moment, Dr. King felt God's presence as
he had never felt it before.

When do I feel closest to God:
in time of need, joy, love, or prayer?

I know not where His islands lift
Their fronded palms in air;
I only know I cannot drift
Beyond His loving care.
JOHN GREENLEAF WHITTIER

WEEK 5
Day 5 _____

"Be still, and know that I am God!"
PSALM 46:10 (NRSV)

The air space in the room in which you
are sitting is alive with hundreds of
television shows. They swirl about invisibly
in living color and exciting sound. This is
not science fiction; it's science fact. But
the only way we can prove this fact is by
means of a "big dish" and a television set.
Just as the air space around you is alive
with an invisible television world, so it is
alive with an invisible faith world. And
just as we need a "big dish" and a
television set to get in touch with the
invisible television world, we need prayer
to get in touch with the invisible faith
world. In other words, prayer is a way to
open our being to contact with the most
real of all worlds: the faith world.

Can I recall a time
since beginning to pray regularly
when I felt in touch
with something beyond this world?
What meditation?

*God exists within us
even more intimately
than we exist within ourselves.*
LOUIS EVELY

*Listen to my words, O LORD,
and hear my sighs.*

PSALM 5:1

An eleventh-century monk, Anselm of
Canterbury, wrote a book called *Proslogion*.
It contains this prayer:
"Lord my God, teach my heart
where and how to seek you,
where and how to find you. . . .
You are my God and you are my Lord,
and I have never seen you.
You have made me and remade me,
and you have bestowed on me
all the good things I possess,
and still I do not know you. . . .
I have not yet done that
for which I was made. . . .
Teach me to seek you . . . for
I cannot seek you unless you teach me or
find you unless you show yourself to me.
Let me seek you in my desire,
let me desire you in my seeking.
Let me find you by loving you,
let me love you when I find you."

How earnestly am I seeking God?

*God is an unutterable sigh,
lying in the depths of the heart.*
SEBASTIAN FRANCK

WEEK 5
Day 7 _____

LORD, . . . you know everything I do.
PSALM 139:1-2

Eddie Rickenbacker and a crew of seven
crashed into the Pacific. They survived
twenty-one days by hand-catching fish,
drinking rain water, and praying. Here's
a prayer they repeated often:
"LORD, . . . you know everything I do. . . .
You see me, whether I am working or
resting; you know all my actions.
Even before I speak,
you already know what I will say.
You are all around me on every side;
you protect me with your power.
Your knowledge of me is too deep;
it is beyond my understanding.
Where could I go to escape from you? . . .
If I flew away beyond the east or
lived in the farthest place in the west,
you would be there to lead me,
you would be there to help me."
PSALM 139:1-7, 9-10

How might I answer this question:
Who is God for me?

The Mighty One
has done great things for me,
and holy is [God's] name.
LUKE 1:49 (NRSV)

WEEKLY MEETING
Sharing Agenda

1 What role did the faith of my parents or guardians play in my own personal faith, especially my faith in God and God's love for me?

2 Can I recall a childhood experience that had a lasting impact on my life? When? What?

3 Can I recall a time when God seemed to help me in a special way? When? How?

4 When do I feel closest to God: in time of need, joy, love, or prayer?

5 Can I recall a time since beginning to pray regularly when I felt in touch with something beyond this world? Which meditation prompted this feeling?

6 On a scale of one (very little) to ten (very much), how earnestly am I seeking God?

7 Who is God for me? How real is God for me right now in my life? How do I explain this?

6   What is God's plan for me?

Coach Grant Teaff of Baylor University
wrote a book entitled *I Believe*. In it he
describes an incident that happened early
in his coaching career.

He and his team were flying back to Texas
on a chartered plane. Suddenly the plane
developed engine trouble. The pilot told
them to prepare for a crash landing.
Minutes later the plane bellied across the
ground, engulfed in a shower of sparks.
Miraculously, no one was hurt.

Later, Coach Teaff knelt and prayed:
"God, I know that you have a plan, a
purpose, and a will for my life and the
lives of these young men. I do not know
what it is, but I'll . . . try to impress upon
the young men I coach this year and
forever that there is more to life than just
playing football; that you do have a
purpose for our lives."

This week's meditations take up the
question of God's purpose in creating you.
The grace you ask for is:

Lord, put into my heart
an unshakeable conviction
that you have a plan for me,
even though I might not yet know it.

Weekly Instruction

Sometimes people become disappointed after a few weeks of meditation. The things they expected to happen did not occur. This brings up an important point. Meditation should not be approached with preconceived notions of what will happen. An example will illustrate why.

You bite into something in the dark, expecting it to be one thing and it isn't. The shock of the unexpected taste almost causes you to spit it out. Meditation can be like that if you approach it with preconceived ideas. Meditation is an exercise of opening yourself to God's grace. And the grace God gives you may be far different—and far better—in the long run than what you expected.

Daily Reading

1	Speak, LORD	1 Sam 3:1-10
2	Love one another	1 Jn 3:11-18
3	Do good to one another	Gal 6:7-10
4	God's surprising choice	1 Cor 1:26-31
5	Power of faith	Heb 11:7-12
6	Our future	1 Jn 3:1-3
7	Shine like stars	Phil 2:12-16

WEEK 6
Day 1

I put my trust in you.
My prayers go up to you;
show me the way I should go.

PSALM 143:8

Doug Alderson graduated from high school
with a lot of unanswered questions. He
got his parents' permission to do a 2,000-
mile hike along the Appalachian Trail
from Maine to Florida. He wanted time to
think about life: Was there a God? What
was the purpose of life? How ought he to
spend his life? Doug wrote later in *Campus
Life* magazine: "I thought the answers
might lie in the beautiful wilderness. . . .
There had to be more to life than money,
TV, parties, and getting high. My hike
was a journey to find myself." Five
months later Doug returned home.
He had found what he was searching for.
There was a God, life had a purpose,
and he had a role to play in it.

When was the last time I went off alone—
like Doug—to seek guidance concerning
the purpose of life and my role in it?
With what results?

Here lies a person who exited the world
without knowing why he entered it.

INSCRIPTION ON A GRAVESTONE

Our love
should not be just words and talk;
it must be true love,
which shows itself in action.

1 JOHN 3:18

Gale Sayers, who played for the Chicago
Bears in the 1960s, was one of the greatest
running backs of all time. Around his neck
he wore a gold medal. On it were inscribed
three words: "I Am Third." Those words
became the title of his best-selling
autobiography. The book explains the
meaning behind the words: "The Lord is
first; my friends are second; and I am
third." Gale is the first to admit that he
doesn't always live up to the motto. But
wearing it around his neck keeps him
from straying too far from it.

Would I be willing to wear Gale's medal
around my neck and make its words my
motto? What changes might I have to
make in my present life if I did?

Ideals are like stars;
you will not succeed
in touching them with your hands.
But . . . following them
you will reach your destiny.

CARL SCHURZ

WEEK 6
Day 3 _____

[Jesus said,]
"I chose you and appointed you
to go and bear much fruit."

JOHN 15:16

Jewish legend explains why God chose
Moses to lead Israel. One day while Moses
was tending sheep, a lamb ran off into the
underbrush. Moses left the others and
pursued it, lest it be killed by a wild
animal. He caught up with it at a stream,
where it was drinking feverishly. When
it had finished, Moses said, "Little one, I
didn't know you ran off because you were
so thirsty. Your tiny legs must be tired."
Then he scooped up the lamb into his
arms and returned to the flock. Seeing
how caring Moses was, God said, "At last
I've found the special person I've been
searching for. I will make Moses shepherd
of my people, Israel."

How do I determine what my future is?
Do I choose it or does God choose me?

Yours are the only hands
with which God can do [God's] work. . . .
Yours are the only eyes
through which God's compassion
can shine upon a troubled world.

SAINT TERESA OF AVILA

God purposely chose . . .
what the world looks down on . . .
in order to destroy
what the world thinks is important.

1 CORINTHIANS 1:27-28

A big-city symphony orchestra played a short concert for a centennial celebration in a small New England town. Next day the townspeople could talk about nothing but the concert. One old-timer said, "All I can say is it was a long way to fetch that big drum just to bang it wunst." At times, we may feel about ourselves the way the old man felt about the drum. We may wonder why God went to all the trouble of creating us. Yet, God's plan would not be complete without us. In fact, each of our roles in God's plan is very important.

Do I ever feel about myself the way the old-timer felt about the drum? Why?

Xvxn though my typxwritxr's old,
it works wxll xxcxpt for onx kxy.
I'vx wishxd many timxs
that it workxd pxrfxctly.
Trux, thxrx'rx 42 kxys that function,
but onx kxy not working
makxs thx diffxrxncx.

AUTHOR UNKNOWN

WEEK 6
Day 5 _____

*[Jesus said,] "If you had faith
as big as a mustard seed,
you could say to this mulberry tree,
'Pull yourself up by the roots
and plant yourself in the sea!'
and it would obey you."*

LUKE 17:6

In the movie *The Empire Strikes Back,*
Luke Skywalker asks the guru Yoda to
help him become a Jedi warrior. Luke
wants to help free the galaxy from the
evil Darth Vader. Yoda starts by teaching
young Luke to lift rocks with his mind.
Then one day Yoda instructs Luke to lift
his X-wing plane out of the swamp where
it is stuck. Luke balks, saying, "Lifting
rocks is one thing; lifting a plane, another."
Predictably, he fails. Then Yoda lifts the
plane easily. Luke exclaims, "I can't
believe it!" Yoda replies, "That's why you
failed!"

How ready am I to commit myself to a
noble cause, as Luke did? How afraid am
I of making the same mistake Luke did?

*Unless there is within us
that which is above us, we shall soon
yield to that which is about us.*

PETER TAYLOR FORSYTH

All things are done
according to God's plan and decision; . . .
God chose us to be [God's] own people . . .
based on what [God] had decided
from the very beginning.

EPHESIANS 1:11

"Calvin and Hobbes" is a cartoon about a
dynamic duo: a little boy and a tiger. One
particular cartoon portrays Calvin saying
something like this: "Paul Gauguin asks:
'Where did I come from? Who am I? And
where am I going?' " Then Calvin answers
Gauguin's question in words like this:
"Well, speaking for myself, I came from
my room. I'm a kid with big plans. And I'm
going outside!" Calvin's lightweight
answers to Gauguin's heavyweight
questions are typical of how many people
today respond to the major questions
about their existence.

What answer would I give
to Gauguin's second and third questions?
How well does my life mirror my answers?

All men should try to learn
before they die
what they are running from, and to,
and why.

JAMES THURBER

70

WEEK 6
Day 7 _____

[Jesus said to his disciples,]
"You are like light for the whole world.
A city built on a hill cannot be hid. . . .
In the same way
your light must shine before people,
so that they will see the good things
you do and praise your Father in heaven."

MATTHEW 5:14, 16

Before the age of electricity, city streets
were lit by gas lamps. Lamplighters lit
these lamps with a flaming torch. One
night an old man stood looking across a
valley to a town on a hillside. He could see
the torch of a lamplighter lighting lamps
as he went. But because of the darkness,
he could not see the lamplighter. He could
see only his torch and the trail of lights
he left behind. The old man said to a friend
standing next to him: "That lamplighter
is a good example of how Christians ought
to live. You may never have known them.
But you know that they passed through
the world by the trail of lights they left
behind."

What trail of lights am I leaving behind?

People may doubt what we say,
but they'll believe what we do.

LEWIS CASS (slightly adapted)

WEEKLY MEETING
Sharing Agenda

1 Do I ever go off by myself to think about the purpose of life and why God created me? What are some answers I have come up with regarding these two questions?

2 To what extent is God first in my life, my friends second, and myself third?

3 How do I discover God's plan for me? Do I choose it in the light of God's plan of salvation? Or does God choose it for me and invite me to live it out?

4 What kind of a self-image do I have? What keeps me from a more positive one—especially in light of the fact that I am created in God's own image?

5 How ready am I to commit myself to a noble cause as Luke Skywalker did? How afraid am I that my faith is not strong enough to support such a commitment?

6 How do I answer Gauguin's second and third questions? How well does my life mirror my answers?

7 If I died tomorrow, what might God say to me about the trail of lights I left behind? What could I say in reply to God?

7 How open am I to God's plan for me?
(Principle and Foundation)

A man and a woman were marooned on a deserted island for years. One day a ship spotted their smoke signal and sent a lifeboat. But instead of rescuing them, the lifeboat crew handed them several newspapers, saying, "The captain wants you to see what's going on in the world before you decide that you want to return to it."

There may be times when you feel like fleeing to a deserted island. But you know you can't. God put you in the world to make it a better place. You have a role to play in God's plan of salvation. But, in the last analysis it is up to you. You can say yes to God's plan and get involved. Or you can say no and do your own thing.

The goal of this week's meditations is to ponder the price you may have to pay if you decide to say yes to God's plan and get involved. The grace you ask before each meditation is:

Lord, put into my heart the desire
to get involved in your plan,
regardless of what it may cost me.

Weekly Instruction

This week's meditations are extremely important. You may wish to ask God's special grace to do them well by making some personal sacrifice, like not eating between meals. This is merely a suggestion. Do what the Spirit moves you to do.

Daily Reading

Recall that the Bible readings are only suggestions. If you decide to do them, read only the chapter and verses indicated. And be sure to pause before and after each reading, as indicated earlier.

Occasionally, a reading from a previous week will be repeated. This is not by mistake but by design.

1 Spiritual athlete   1 Cor 9:24-27
2 Vine and branches   Jn 15:1-17
3 Sole goal   Phil 3:7-11
4 Keep knocking   Lk 11:5-8
5 Lasting crown   2 Cor 4:16-18
6 Remarkable paradox   2 Cor 6:5-10
7 Wealthy youth   Mt 19:16-24

WEEK 7
Day 1 _____

Every athlete in training
submits to strict discipline,
in order to be crowned with a wreath
that will not last; . . .
we do it for one that will last forever.

1 CORINTHIANS 9:25

In his autobiography, titled *Nigger,* Dick
Gregory, the athlete, comedian, and social
activist, tells how he disciplined his body
to run for hours each day—even in winter.
He writes: "I don't think
I would ever have finished high school
without running. I never got hungry
while I was running, even though
we never ate breakfast at home and
I didn't always have enough money
for lunch. . . . I was proud of my body . . .
and never had to take a rest."
Dick Gregory is a living example of what
Paul talks about in today's reading.

To what extent am I pursuing
the perishable wreath of this life
with more effort and resolve than I am
the imperishable wreath of eternal life?

What most people tend to forget
is that we have unbelievable control
over our destiny.

BILL GOVE

*[Jesus said,] "Whoever remains in me,
and I in him, will bear much fruit."*
JOHN 15:5

A woman was touring a piano factory.
First, the guide showed her a room where
workers were sawing wood. Next, the
guide took her into a room where workers
were building piano frames. Then, the
guide took her into a room where workers
were sanding and varnishing the piano
frames. Next, the woman visited a room
where workers were fitting metal strings
and ivory keys into the frames. Finally,
the woman came to the showroom, where
a musician was seated at a piano playing
beautiful music. Afterward the woman
thought: The difference between what I
saw in the first room and in the last room
is the difference between an acorn and a
tree. It is the difference between what I
am now and what I can become.

In which of the five rooms referred to
above am I in my spiritual journey?
Is anything in particular tending to
hold up or delay my spiritual progress?

*Alas for those who never sing,
but die with their music within them.*
OLIVER WENDELL HOLMES

WEEK 7
Day 3 _____

The LORD said to me,
"I chose you before I gave you life,
and before you were born
I selected you."

JEREMIAH 1:4-5

Imagine you are about to be born into the world. God calls you and offers you two lives on earth to choose from. God's first choice involves a short life of sickness, poverty, and ridicule by people. This is the best way you can accomplish the task God has in mind for you. God's second choice is just the opposite. It involves a long life of health, wealth, and honor. God tells you, however, that God will love you deeply regardless of your choice. Realizing the hard decision that is being presented, God asks if you want to take a few days to think about it before deciding. On the other hand, God wants you to be honest. Would thinking about your decision for a few days be a formality, because you would probably end up picking the second option anyway?

How open would I be
to God's first choice for me? Explain.

Today's decision is tomorrow's reality.

AUTHOR UNKNOWN

[Jesus said,]
"The Kingdom of heaven is like this.
A man happens to find a treasure
hidden in a field. . . .
He goes and sells everything he has . . .
and buys that field."

MATTHEW 13:44

A magazine ran a story about teenagers who belong to the Santa Clara Swimming Club. They get up at 5:30 A.M. and hurry through the chilly air to an outdoor pool. There they swim for two hours. After a shower and a bite to eat, they dash off to school. After school they return to the pool for two more hours. Then they hurry home, eat, hit the books, and fall into bed, exhausted. The next morning the alarm rings at 5:30, and they start all over again. When asked why she sacrifices so much to swim, one girl said: "My goal is to make the Olympic team. If going to parties hurts that, then why go? The more miles I swim, the better. Sacrifice is the thing."

What is my main goal right now?
How generously am I sacrificing
to reach it?

The enemy of the best is not the worst,
but the good enough. L. P. JACKS

*What can I offer the LORD
for all [the LORD's] goodness to me?*

PSALM 116:12

The Spiritual Exercises of Saint Ignatius
present a set of guidelines for living.
They go like this: "I believe that I was
created to share my life and love with God
and other people, forever. I believe that
God created all other things to help me
achieve this goal. I believe, therefore, that
I should use the other things God created
insofar as they help me attain my goal and
abstain from them insofar as they hinder
me. It follows, therefore, that I should not
prefer certain things to others. That is, I
should not value, automatically, health
over sickness, wealth over poverty, honor
over dishonor, or a long life over a short
one. I believe my sole norm for valuing
and preferring a thing should be this: How
well does it help me attain the end for
which I was created?"

Would I be willing to adopt this statement
as a guide for my life?
If not, how would I reword it
to make it acceptable?

Life is God's novel. Let God write it.

ISAAC BASHEVIS SINGER

*What seems to be God's foolishness
is wiser than human wisdom.*
1 CORINTHIANS 1:25

The following reflection was found in the
pocket of a dead Confederate soldier:
"I asked for health
that I might do greater things;
I was given infirmity,
that I might do better things. . . .
I asked for riches, that I might be happy;
I was given poverty,
that I might be wise. . . .
I asked for power,
that I might have the praise of men;
I was given weakness,
that I might feel the need of God. . . .
I got nothing I asked for,
but everything I hoped for.
Almost despite myself,
my unspoken prayers were answered.
I am among all men most richly blessed."

What is the point of this reflection?
How does it relate to the "guidelines for
living" of the previous meditation?

*Troubles are often the means God uses
to fashion people
into something better than they are.*
ANONYMOUS

WEEK 7
Day 7 _____

*[Jesus prayed to his Father,] "Not my
will . . . but your will be done."*
LUKE 22:42

"I asked God to take away my pride /
and God said, 'No,' / He said it was not
for Him to take away, / but for me
to give up. / I asked God to make my
handicapped child whole, / and God said,
'No.' / He said, 'Her spirit is whole, /
her body is only temporary.' /
I asked God to grant me patience,
and God said, 'No.' / He said that
patience is a by-product of tribulation. /
It isn't granted, it is earned. /
I asked God to give me happiness,
and God said, 'No.' / He said he gives
blessings; / happiness is up to me. /
I asked God to spare my pain, /
and God said, 'No.' / He said, 'Suffering
draws you apart from worldly cares /
and brings you closer to me.' . . . /
I asked God to help me love others
as much as he loves me, and God said,
'Ah, finally you have the idea.' "
AUTHOR UNKNOWN

Reread the poem, savoring each thought.

*When I will what God wills,
I know my heart is right.*

WEEKLY MEETING
Sharing Agenda

Try writing out your response to some of
the questions below for sharing with the
group. Many people find this helpful. So
do group members.

1 Am I pursuing the perishable wreath
   of this life more earnestly than I am
   the imperishable wreath of eternal life?
   How do I justify this?

2 Is any obstacle in particular arresting
   my spiritual progress? If so, how might
   I overcome it?

3 On a scale of one (closed) to ten (totally
   open), how open am I to God's first
   choice referred to in Day 3?

4 What is my chief goal right now? What
   is the chief sacrifice I am making to
   reach it? What is my motivation for the
   sacrifice?

5 How ready am I to adopt the "guidelines
   for living" referred to in Day 5? How
   do I explain this?

6 How do I interpret the reflection found
   in the dead soldier's pocket? How do I
   see it related to the "guidelines for
   living"?

7 How ready am I to hand God a blank
   check and allow God to fill it out for
   me? How do I explain this?

8   How aware am I of sin's presence in my life?

The images on a television screen owe their existence to the television set. When it goes on, they go on. When it goes off, they go off. Suppose the images decided to rebel and said to the set, "We don't need you anymore. We declare our independence from you." Such a declaration would be ludicrous. It would be like an echo telling a voice, "I declare my independence from you. I don't need you."

In a sense, that's what sin is. It is an attempt to declare our independence from God. To put it in another way, it is saying no to God and God's plan for us.

This week's meditations put you in touch with the power of sin—a power that can destroy you and the world. The grace you ask before each meditation is:

Lord, enlighten my mind
to see my sinfulness.
Move my heart
to be sickened by what I see.
Touch my soul
to cry out in shame and sorrow.

Weekly Instruction

You may wish to recite the following
ancient prayer at the end of each meditation,
just before you say the Lord's Prayer:

Soul of Christ, sanctify me.
Body of Christ, save me.
Blood of Christ, inebriate me.
Water from the side of Christ, wash me.
Passion of Christ, strengthen me.
O Good Jesus, hear me.
Within thy wounds hide me.
Permit me not to be separated from thee.
From the wicked foe defend me.
At the hour of death call me
and bid me come to thee,
that with all the saints I may praise thee
for ever and ever. Amen.

This week you might also consider
celebrating the sacrament of Reconciliation.
You may even feel moved to make a
"general confession" of your life. If so, ask
a priest how to do it.

Daily Reading

1	All show, no soul	Mt 23:1–12
2	How it started	Gen 3:1–3
3	I have sinned	Ps 51:1–13
4	Sin upon sin	Amos 2:6–8
5	Whitewashed tombs	Mt 23:23–28
6	All have sinned	Ps 14
7	Loving forgiveness	Ps 32

WEEK 8
Day 1 _____

"Take to heart these words."
DEUTERONOMY 6:6 (NAB)

"If you get what you want in your struggle for self, / And the world makes you king for a day, / Just go to the mirror and look at yourself, / And see what that man has to say. / For it isn't your father, or mother, or brother, / Who upon you their judgment will pass. / The fellow whose verdict counts most in your life / Is the one staring back from the glass. . . . / He's the fellow to please—never mind all the rest! / For he's with you right up to the end. / And you've passed your most difficult dangerous test, / If the man in the glass is your friend. / You may fool the world down the pathway of years, / And get pats on the back, as you pass, / But your final reward will be headache or tears, / If you've cheated the man in the glass."

AUTHOR UNKNOWN

What is one way I might be in danger of cheating "the man in the glass"?

*No man can produce great things
who is not thoroughly sincere
in dealing with himself.*
JAMES RUSSELL LOWELL

My sins have caught up with me,
and I can no longer see.

PSALM 40:12

Years ago there was a popular television
program called "The Mork and Mindy
Show." Mork was an alien who had
remarkable power. One day he shared
some of this power with a few of his
friends on earth. Touching his fingertips
to theirs, he transferred just a little bit to
them. Right away they began using it to
make people do ridiculous things, like turn
cartwheels and leap up and down. Mork
was horrified and shouted, "Stop! You're
misusing the power. Give it back!" That
episode is a good illustration of what sin
is. It's misusing the power and talents
that God has shared with us.

How aware am I of misusing God's gifts
and talents? What are some concrete
examples of how I have done this?

My sense of sin
is linked to my sense of God.
The closer I am to God,
the more aware I am of my sinfulness.
This is because distance from God
reduces the contrast necessary for me
to recognize my true condition.

WEEK 8
Day 3 _____

*Create a pure heart in me, O God,
and put a new and loyal spirit in me.*

PSALM 51:10

Thomas Merton had just graduated from
high school and was touring Europe alone.
One night in his room, Tom underwent a
soul-stirring experience. It made him
deeply aware of all the sinfulness in his
life. He wrote later in *The Seven Storey
Mountain:* "My whole being rose up in
revolt and horror with what was within
me, and my soul desired escape . . . from
all this with an intensity and urgency
unlike anything I had ever known before.
And now I think for the first time in my
whole life I really began to pray . . .
praying to the God I had never known, to
reach down towards me out of [God's]
darkness and help me to get free of the
thousand terrible things that held my will
in their slavery."

What is the closest I have ever come
to having an experience like this?

*It is one thing to mourn for sin
because it exposes us to hell,
and another to mourn for it
because it is an infinite evil.*

GARDINER SPRING

"They sell into slavery honest men. . . .
They trample down the weak . . .
and push the poor out of the way."

AMOS 2:6-7

You'd hardly expect the dean of American
psychiatry to talk about sin. But that's
what Dr. Karl Menninger does in his book
Whatever Became of Sin? He is troubled
by individuals who won't admit that they
sin. He is also troubled by "sins of
collective responsibility"—sins committed
by groups or nations, such as disregard
of the poor, pollution of the environment,
exploitation of migrant workers. The
tragic thing about "sins of collective
responsibility," says Dr. Menninger, is
that single individuals don't consider
themselves responsible for them.

How hard is it for me to admit that I sin?
How responsible do I feel
for "sins of collective responsibility"?

We're improving immensely.
We don't steal anymore; we only "lift."
We don't lie; we only "misinform."
We don't fornicate; we only "fool around."
We don't kill;
we only "terminate a pregnancy."

ANONYMOUS

WEEK 8
Day 5 _____

If we say that we have no sin . . .
we make a liar out of God.

1 JOHN 1:8, 10

In the book *In His Presence*, Louis Evely
writes: "The worst evil lies not in
committing evil but in committing evil
while pretending it is good. . . .
It is better to sin with sincerity than
to lie to oneself in order to stay virtuous.
You will repent of a straightforward sin
more easily than one wrapped in doubt.
Don't muddy the water so as to fish
from it whatever you desire." Then in
a burst of emotion, Evely concludes:
"Commit straightforward, clear-cut and
undeniable sins of which you will later
be able to repent with the same sincerity
you use in committing them. . . .
If you are weak enough to sin,
do not be too proud to recognize the fact."

What advice would I give to people
who find it hard to admit that they sin?

There are two kinds of people:
the righteous
who believe themselves sinners;
the rest
who believe themselves righteous.

BLAISE PASCAL

My sins have caught up with me,
and I can no longer see. . . .
I have lost my courage.

PSALM 40:12

In your imagination, replay what went
on in the minds and hearts of the first
woman and the first man after they
sinned. Try to visualize all the pain and
suffering that their sin unleashed in the
world. Pass in review all the people who
have sinned since the time of the first sin.
Consider how their sins have added to the
suffering of the world. Stand appalled at
what sin is: not only a rejection of God
and God's plan for us, but also an
instrument of suffering and destruction.
In your mind's eyes, see Jesus hanging on
the cross—suffering because of sin. Finally,
speak to Jesus about why he suffered all
this pain. Then ponder these three
questions:

What have I done for Jesus in the past?
What am I doing for Jesus now?
What ought I to do for Jesus
in the future?

O Lord, reform our world—
beginning with me.

A CHINESE CHRISTIAN'S PRAYER

WEEK 8
Day 7 _____

*"We are healed
by the punishment he suffered,
made whole by the blows he received."*

ISAIAH 53:5

We all need to admit two things to
ourselves. First, that we are sinners.
Second, that in spite of this, our Father
in heaven loves us. Julian of Norwich, the
great English mystic, explains that even
past sins can be turned into something
good—if we acknowledge them as sins.
Julian says, for example: "If we never fell,
we should never know how weak and
wretched we are in ourselves; nor should
we appreciate the astonishing love of our
Maker. . . . We sin grievously, yet despite
all this . . . we are no less precious in
[God's] sight. By the simple fact that
we fall, we gain knowledge of what God's
love means."

To what extent have I experienced
what Julian of Norwich refers to?

*Voice of Jesus, you called me
when I strayed from you.
Arms of Jesus, you raised me
when I slipped and fell.
Heart of Jesus, you loved me
even when I sinned.*

WEEKLY MEETING
Sharing Agenda

1 What is one way that I tend to cheat "the man in the glass"?

2 What is one gift from God that I tend to misuse? Why this one?

3 What is the closest I have ever come to having an experience like Merton's?

4 How hard is it for me to admit my failures, shortcomings, and sinfulness?

5 What advice would I give to people who were finding it hard to admit to their sinfulness?

6 What have I done for Jesus in the past? What am I doing for Jesus now? What ought I to do for Jesus in the future?

7 To what extent have I experienced what Julian of Norwich refers to?

9 How aware am I that I will be held accountable for my life?

One day a shabbily dressed man stood on a busy Chicago street corner. As office workers filed by on their way to lunch, he'd raise his arm, point to the nearest one, and shout, "Guilty!" Then he'd lower his arm for a minute or two and go through the whole procedure again.

The effect on the office workers was eerie. They'd glance at the man, look away, glance back, and hurry on.

Humorous as the story is, it makes an important point: Like every living person, each of us is guilty of sin and will someday be judged by God. This week's meditations focus on this reality. The grace you ask before each meditation is:

Lord,
help me live in such a way now
that I'll rejoice in your judgment later.

Weekly Instruction

Spiritual directors recommend that you get into the habit of performing a daily "judgment" of your actions. One way to do this is to take three minutes each night to do the following:

First minute. Replay your day. Pick out a high point in it—a good thing you did, like going out of your way to help someone. Then talk to God about it, giving thanks for the opportunity to do it.

Second minute. Replay your day again. This time pick out a low point—a bad thing you did, like putting down someone who really needs to be lifted up. Then talk to Jesus about it, asking forgiveness for responding as you did.

Third minute. Look ahead to tomorrow to a critical point—a hard thing you must do, like dealing with a personal problem. Then talk to the Holy Spirit about the problem, asking help to deal with it.

Daily Reading

1	Rich fool	Lk 12:13-21
2	Two options	Ps 1
3	Deeds: good/bad	1 Tim 5:24-25
4	Parable of coins	Lk 19:11-27
5	Parable of weeds	Mt 13:36-43
6	Parable of net	Mt 13:47-50
7	Sheep and goats	Mt 25:31-46

WEEK 9
Day 1 _____

Everyone must die . . .
and after that be judged by God.

HEBREWS 9:27

There's an ancient play called *Everyman*.
It opens with a "Messenger" stepping out
in front of the curtain, looking intently at
the audience, and saying, "I pray you . . .
hear this matter with reverence. . . . Look
well, and take heed. . . . For ye shall hear
how our Heavenly King calleth Everyman
to a general reckoning." The play then
portrays Death coming to tell Everyman
that his earthly years are over and it is
time for him to enter eternity. When
Everyman recovers from shock, he asks
Death to give him time to ask his three
most-cherished earthly companions—
Power, Prestige, and Pleasure—to enter
eternity with him. Death obliges. To
Everyman's dismay, however, they refuse
to go with him.

Can I name three "most-cherished earthly
companions" of my own who will refuse
to enter eternity with me?

The few little years we spend on earth
are only the first scene in a Divine Drama
that extends into eternity.

EDWIN MARKHAM

Every one of us, then,
will have to give an account . . . to God.
ROMANS 14:12

The hero in the novel *The Man Who Lost Himself* trails a suspect to a Paris hotel. To learn the suspect's room number without arousing suspicion, the hero gives the clerk his own name and asks if a man by that name is registered. While the clerk checks the room list, the hero plans to watch for the suspect's number. To the hero's surprise, the clerk doesn't check the list. He simply says, "He's in room 40; he's expecting you." The hero follows the bellhop to room 40. When the door opens, he sees a man who is his double, except that he's heavier and older. It is the hero himself, twenty years in the future. The story is science fiction, but it contains an important truth: There's a person in everyone's future. It is the person we are becoming.

What kind of person am I becoming? How sure am I of this?

The great thing in this world
is not so much where we are,
but in what direction we are moving.
OLIVER WENDELL HOLMES

WEEK 9
Day 3 _____

Final judgment
must wait until the Lord comes. . . .
And then everyone will receive from God
the praise he deserves.

1 CORINTHIANS 4:5

John was a contractor for a construction
company. To increase his personal income,
he routinely cheated on materials that
went into the homes he built. He was so
adept at concealing his shortcuts that he
joked to a close friend that even he
couldn't detect them once they had been
made. John's last construction project
before retiring was the one he cheated on
most. It was supposed to be a luxury
home. Even John worried that he had gone
too far this time. Imagine his shock when
the company gave him this house as a gift
for his years of service.

How is this story a parable of life?
What is one shortcut I could get away with
in what I am currently doing?
Why don't I take it?

First we form habits,
then they form us.
Conquer your bad habits,
or they'll eventually conquer you.

DR. ROB GILBERT

*"[The Lord] took note of all my sins
and tied them all together;
[The Lord] hung them around my neck,
and I grew weak beneath the weight."*

LAMENTATIONS 1:14

There's a moving story that has survived
the centuries. It's about Pietri Bandinelli,
an attractive young man with clear eyes
and a kind face. Leonardo da Vinci chose
him to be his Jesus model for his painting
The Lord's Supper. Years later, Leonardo
had not yet completed the painting. One
day, however, the spirit moved him, and
he went to the slums of Milan to look for
his Judas model. After an hour, he found
the perfect man. His eyes were cloudy; his
face was harsh. Later, while the man was
posing, Leonardo asked him, "Have we
met before?" The man said, "Yes, I was
your Jesus model. But much has changed
in my life since then."

What is the story's point? What lesson
might I draw from it for my own life?

*I coulda had class.
I coulda been a contender.
I coulda been somebody.
Instead of a bum, which is what I am.*

ACTOR MARLON BRANDO in *On the Waterfront*

WEEK 9
Day 5 _____

*There is nothing
that can be hid from God. . . .
And it is to [God]
that we must all give an account.*
HEBREWS 4:13

In April 1987, baseball Hall of Famer
Mickey Mantle took sick on a plane and
was rushed from the airport to a hospital.
Later, Mickey told an Associated Press
reporter about a dream he had in the
hospital. He said, "I dreamed I died and
went to heaven. Saint Peter greeted me
and I said, 'I'm Mickey Mantle!' He said,
'Really?'. . . I went in to see God, and God
said, 'We can't keep you here because of
the way you acted. But do me a favor and
sign six dozen baseballs.' " When the
humor of Mantle's dream subsides, the
truth of it emerges. No one will escape
God's judgment. And no one will get
VIP treatment.

What is one concern I sometimes have
about God's judgment after I die?

*When the One Great Scorer comes
To write against your name,
He writes—not that you won or lost—
But how you played the game.*
GRANTLAND RICE

*The sins of some people are plain to see,
and their sins
go ahead of them to judgment.*

1 TIMOTHY 5:24

Dr. Wilder Penfield of Montreal's
Neurological Institute has made an amazing
discovery. *Time* magazine reported it this
way: "Surgeon Wilder Penfield . . . by
chance found brain sites that when
stimulated electrically led one patient to
hear an old tune . . . and still another to
relive the experience of having her baby."
Penfield's findings convince some scientists
that every action of our life is recorded in
our brain. Penfield also found that our
feelings about our actions at the time we
did them (were they good or evil?) are also
recorded. In other words, there is now
solid physiological support for the biblical
teaching of judgment after death.

Albert Camus once said,
"I shall tell you a secret, my friend.
Do not wait for the last judgment.
It takes place every day."
What point was Camus making?

*God will not look you over for medals,
degrees, or diplomas, but scars.*

ELBERT HUBBARD

WEEK 9
Day 7 _____

*All [the dead] were judged
according to what they had done.*
REVELATION 20:13

Saint George's chapel in London was built
as a memorial to air-raid victims in World
War II. In the chapel are four large books
containing the names of over 60,000
victims. One page of one book lies open at
a time. Each day the page is turned to a
new set of names. As you read a name on
the page, you have no way of knowing if
that person was rich or poor, ugly or fair.
Nor does it matter. All that matters is
what the person did with the time allotted
him or her by God. Poet Phyllis McGinley
says: "When I was seven . . . I wanted to
be a tight-rope dancer. . . . At fifteen my
ambition was the stage. Now in my
sensitive declining years I would give
anything . . . to be a saint."

How have my goals and ambitions changed
over the years? If I could begin
my life over, what is one change
I would consider making? Why?

*It is not only what we do,
but also what we do not do,
for which we are held accountable.*
MOLIERE

WEEKLY MEETING
Sharing Agenda

1 Can I name three "earthly companions"—like Everyman's Power, Prestige, and Pleasure—whom I value highly right now, but who will decline to enter eternity with me? How do I feel about this?

2 To what extent am I more helpful and forgiving today than I was a year ago? Examples?

3 What is one shortcut I could get away with in what I am currently doing? What keeps me from taking it?

4 What is one point (symbolic or otherwise) that the story of Pietri Bandinelli makes?

5 On a scale of one (hardly any) to ten (very big), what impact does the thought of a judgment after death have on my daily actions? How do I explain this?

6 What is Albert Camus's point, and how does it shed light on the nature of judgment after death?

7 Have my goals and ambitions been affected in any way since I began meditating regularly? How? If I could begin my life over, what is one change I'd make in the way I have approached life up to this point?

10 How does the thought of death impact the way I live?

The famous French aviator Antoine de Saint-Exupéry was forced down in the Sahara, a thousand miles from civilization. He had only a meager water supply.

Repairing his damaged engine, with one eye on his vanishing water supply, Saint-Exupéry came face-to-face with death. Like two boxers, they stared at each other, eyeball-to-eyeball.

Saint-Exupéry's close brush with death reminds us of John McLelland's words in *The Clown and the Crocodile:* "One day a group of people will go to a cemetery, hold a brief service, and return home. All except one; that will be you."

"It's too bad that dying is the last thing we do," says Robert Herhold, "because it could teach us so much about life."

This week's meditations focus on death. The grace you ask of God before each daily meditation is:

Lord,
teach me about death,
that it may teach me about life.

Weekly Instruction

A problem you might experience after meditating for some months is dryness. It consists in finding it hard to pray. You feel that nothing is happening or that God seems miles away.

The cause of dryness can range all the way from spiritual negligence or sin to physical or mental stress. Sometimes God allows it to happen—or uses it—to deepen your faith and fidelity.

The temptation to cut your meditation short when dryness occurs should be resisted. In fact, some spiritual directors recommend extending your meditation a few minutes longer when you experience dryness.

Daily Reading

1	Many rooms	Jn 14:1-6
2	Be prepared	Mt 25:1-13
3	God gives/God takes	Job 1:13-22
4	Widow's son	Lk 7:11-17
5	Back to dust	Ps 90:1-6
6	Home in heaven	2 Cor 5:1-10
7	I fear no evil	Ps 23

WEEK 10
Day 1

[Jesus said,]
"Believe in God and believe also in me.
There are many rooms
in my Father's house, and I am going
to prepare a place for you. . . .
I will come back and take you to myself,
so that you will be where I am."

JOHN 14:1-3

A king gave his favorite jester a magic wand, saying, "Keep this until you find a fool bigger than yourself." Years later the king lay dying. He called his favorite jester and said, "I'm going on a long journey." The jester asked, "Where to?" The king replied, "I'm not sure!" The jester said, "When will you return?" The king replied, "Never!" "Are you prepared for the journey?" the jester asked. "Not at all," answered the king. "Then take this magic wand," said the jester. "It belongs to you."

How prepared am I for the journey the king is referring to? What could I tell God about my preparedness for death?

There is no death!
The stars go down
to rise on some fairer shore.

J. L. McCREERY

*"God said to him,
'You fool! This very night
you will have to give up your life.' "*

LUKE 12:20

Three student devils were preparing to go to earth for some on-the-job training. The teacher asked them what strategy they had decided to use to get people to sin. The first devil said, "I think I'll use the tried-and-true approach. I'll tell people, 'There's no God, so enjoy life.' " The teacher nodded approvingly. Then he turned to the second devil and said, "What about you?" The second devil said, "I think I'll use a more up-to-date approach. I'll tell people, 'There's no hell, so enjoy life.' " Again, the teacher nodded approvingly. Then he turned to the third devil and said, "What about you?" The third devil said, "I think I'll use a more down-to-earth approach. I'll simply tell people, 'There's no hurry, so enjoy life.' "

Which approach tempts me most?

*I can't be prepared for death too soon,
because I can't be sure
when too soon will be too late.*

ANONYMOUS

WEEK 10
Day 3

"Listen! I am coming like a thief!"
REVELATION 16:15

A merchant in ancient Baghdad sent his servant to the market to buy supplies. Minutes later the servant returned, trembling. He said, "Master! Master! As I walked through the market, I was jostled by someone in the crowd. When I looked up, I saw it was Death. He peered at me threateningly. Lend me your fastest horse that I may flee to far-off Samarra. He will never think of looking for me there." The merchant obliged. Then the merchant went to the market. Lo and behold, who should he see but Death. "Why did you give my servant such a threatening look?" the merchant asked. "That wasn't a threatening look," said Death. "It was a look of surprise. I was amazed to see your servant here in Baghdad. For I had a date with him tonight in far-off Samarra."

How would I react if I learned
I had a date with death tonight?

The dark background
which death supplies
brings out the tender colors of life
in all their purity.

GEORGE SANTAYANA

*[Jesus said,] "The sorrow in my heart
is so great that it almost crushes me."*
MATTHEW 26:38

Al Dewlen was standing over a messy
workbench, trying to decide what job to
do before supper. Suddenly he heard his
name. He looked up and saw his wife and
the pastor of his church. Al's jaw dropped.
"What's wrong?" he asked. "Mike's dead,"
his wife said. Instantly, Al lost contact
with reality. His mind flashed back across
the years. First, he saw his son Mike
playing Little League baseball. Next, he
saw him as captain of the high school's
football team. Finally, he saw him in his
Marine uniform. Mike was a son he was
truly proud of. Al said later, "The news
left me so shocked that I was unable to
speak to my wife or even take her in my
arms."

Can I imagine my family's reaction
to my death?

The gardener asked,
"Who plucked this flower?"
The Master said,
"I plucked it for myself,"
and the gardener held his peace.
CHILD'S GRAVESTONE IN ENGLAND

WEEK 10
Day 5

What can we take out of the world?
1 TIMOTHY 6:7

In *As You Like It,* William Shakespeare
reviews the seven ages of life: "At first the
infant, / Mewling and puking in the
nurse's arms. . . . / Then the whining
school-boy, with his satchel / And shining
morning face, creeping like snail /
Unwillingly to school. / And then the
lover, / Sighing like furnace, with a
woeful ballad. . . . / Then a soldier, / Full
of strange oaths . . . / Seeking the bubble
reputation. . . . / And then the justice . . .
/ With eyes severe and beard of formal
cut. . . . / The sixth age shifts / Into the
lean and slipper'd pantaloon . . . and his
big manly voice, / Turning again toward
childish treble, pipes / And whistles in his
sound. / Last scene of all, / That ends this
strange eventful history, / Is second
childishness, and mere oblivion, /
Sans teeth, sans eyes, sans tastes,
sans everything."

How do I interpret Shakespeare's point
in describing life as he does?

*Why should a man certain of immortality
think of his life at all?*

JOSEPH CONRAD

This is how it will be
when the dead are raised to life.
1 CORINTHIANS 15:42

Henry van Dyke portrays death this way:
"I am standing upon the seashore. A ship
at my side spreads her white sails to the
morning breeze and starts for the blue
ocean. She is an object of beauty and
strength, and I stand and watch until at
last she hangs like a speck of white cloud
just where the sea and sky come down to
mingle with each other. Then someone at
my side says, 'There! She's gone!' Gone
where? Gone from my sight, that is all.
She is just as large in mast and hull and
spar as she was when she left my side and
just as able to bear her load of living
freight to the place of destination.
Her diminished size is in me, not in her.
And just at the moment when someone
at my side says, 'There she goes!'
there are eyes watching her coming
and other voices ready to take up
the glad shout, 'Here she comes!' "

How do I understand van Dyke's parable?

Ever notice how everybody wants to go
to heaven and nobody wants to die?
AUTHOR UNKNOWN

WEEK 10
Day 7 _____

"Father!
In your hands I place my spirit!"
LUKE 23:46

In *Through the Valley of the Kwai,* Ernest
Gordon describes the death of a young
prisoner of war. At first, the youth
struggled with the idea of death. Gordon
writes: "I had brought my Bible with me
. . . and in the dim light of the hut I began
to read. . . . 'Yea, though I walk through
the valley of the shadow of death, I will
fear no evil: for thou art with me; thy rod
and thy staff comfort me.' " When Gordon
finished reading, he looked at the dying
youth. He writes: "His gray eyes were far
away. He was listening within himself—
to the message those words had brought."
Then the boy turned to Gordon and said
with perfect calm, "Everything is going
to be all right." The boy was now ready
to meet his Lord.

In my mind's eye, how do I image
the kind of death I would like to have?

I'm not afraid to die, honey. . . .
I know the Lord
has his arms wrapped around
this big, fat sparrow.
SINGER ETHEL WATERS

WEEKLY MEETING
Sharing Agenda

1 What was my closest call with death? When? Where? How?

2 How prepared was I for death at that time? How prepared would I be if I were to die in five minutes?

3 If I learned I was to die in five minutes, who/what would I miss leaving behind most? Why?

4 Which family member would I choose to say good-bye to if I could choose only one? What message would I give him or her for the others?

5 What is Shakespeare's point in his review of the "seven ages of life"? Why do I think God designed life that way?

6 When I think of death, do I tend to view it primarily as leaving earth or as going to God? Why?

7 Have I ever been present at a death of someone? Who? When? What struck me most about the experience?

11 How conscious am I of God's forgiveness of me?

Richard Pindell wrote a short story called "Somebody's Son." It opens with a runaway boy writing a letter home to his mother. He expresses the hope that his old-fashioned father will forgive him and accept him again as his son. The boy writes:

"In a few days I'll be passing our property. If Dad'll take me back, ask him to tie a white cloth on the apple tree in the field next to our house."

Days later the boy is seated on a train, rapidly approaching his house. Soon the tree will be visible around the next bend. But the boy can't bring himself to look at it. He's afraid the white cloth won't be there. Turning to the man sitting next to him, he says, nervously, "Mister, will you do me a favor? Around the bend on the right, you'll see a tree. See if there's a white cloth tied to it."

As the train rumbles past the tree, the boy stares straight ahead. Then in a quaking voice he asks, "Mister, is a white cloth tied to one of the branches of the tree?"

The man answers in a surprised voice, "Why, son, there's a white cloth tied to practically every branch!"

That story is a parable of God's great forgiveness of us. This week's meditations focus on this forgiveness. The grace you ask for is:

Lord, help me see
that there is a wideness in your mercy
like the wideness of the sea.

Weekly Instruction

Week 8 noted that the Holy Spirit might inspire you to desire to celebrate the sacrament of Reconciliation. If that didn't happen then, be attentive to any movement of the Holy Spirit this week.

Daily Reading

1	Quick to forgive	Is 55:3-11
2	Quick to understand	Jn 8:1-11
3	Seventy times seven	Mt 18:21-35
4	Give me a new spirit	Ps 51:1-10
5	You have set me free	Rom 6:15-23
6	You forgave my sins	Ps 32:1-7
7	The restored son	Lk 15:11-24

WEEK 11
Day 1 _____

"How can I give you up?"
HOSEA 11:8

The prophet Hosea speaks of God's love
and forgiveness in a touching way.
Speaking in God's name, he says:
"When *Israel* was a child, I loved *him* and
called *him* out of Egypt. . . .
But the more I called to *him*,
the more *he* turned away from me. . . .
Yet I was the one
who taught *Israel* to walk. . . .
How can I abandon *[Israel]*? . . .
My heart will not let me do it!
My love for *you* is too strong.
I will not punish *you* in my anger. . . .
For I am God and not man.
I, the Holy One, am with *you*.
I will not come to *you* in anger."

HOSEA 11:1-3, 8-9

How does this passage impact me
when I reread it in a whisper,
imagining that God is saying my name
in place of the words in italics
(referring to Israel)?

*[LORD,] your goodness and love
will be with me all my life;
and your house will be my home
as long as I live.*

PSALM 23:6

*"Can a woman forget her own baby
and not love the child she bore?
Even if a mother should forget her child,
I will never forget you."*

ISAIAH 49:15

A woman dropped a beautiful orange vase on the floor; it splintered into dozens of pieces. She swept them up and threw them into the wastebasket. An hour later she found her little daughter had retrieved the pieces and had pasted them on a piece of cardboard. Then, using a green crayon, she had drawn stems and leaves on each piece, converting them into a bouquet of lovely flowers. The woman was moved to tears. Where she had seen trash, her daughter had seen treasure. In a similar way, God retrieves us from the wastebasket of sin and fashions us into something beautiful.

Do I know someone who is messed up but who has a treasure inside? How might I help this person bring it forth?

*The human race would be vastly poorer
if it had not been for men and women
who were willing to take risks
against the longest odds.*

BERNARD BARUCH (slightly adapted)

WEEK 11
Day 3 _____

"I will forgive their sins and
I will no longer remember their wrongs.
I, the LORD, have spoken."

JEREMIAH 31:34

One of the strangest plays in Rose Bowl
history occurred in 1929 on New Year's
Day. California's Roy Riegels picked up a
Georgia Tech fumble and ran it back
sixty-five yards in the wrong direction.
His own players eventually tackled him.
When California tried to punt, Tech
blocked the kick and scored a safety,
Tech's ultimate margin of victory. At
halftime, Riegels expected the worst from
Coach Price. But Price didn't mention the
wrong-way run. When halftime was over,
Price put his hand on Roy's shoulder and
said, "The game's only half over. Give it
your all!" Roy did.

Price's forgiveness of Roy and
God's forgiveness of me invite me to ask,
How forgiving am I when someone crushes
one of my dreams as Roy did Price's dream
of a Rose Bowl victory?

Forgiveness
is the fragrance the violet sheds
on the heel that crushed it.

MARK TWAIN

Remove my sin, and I will be clean.
PSALM 51:7

A newspaper columnist wrote about a
program for removing tattoos—especially
gang-related ones—from young people.
A surprising thing then happened.
Thousands of letters came in from people
all over the country for more information
on the program. Because of the remarkable
response, the Los Angeles School District
and a local cable television company
produced a film called *Untattoo You.* It
told about the dangers of amateur tattooing
and showed how difficult it is to remove
tattoos. The stars of the film were the
young people themselves. They talked
frankly about why they were tattooed in
the first place and why they now wanted
the tattoos removed.

We've all done things we'd like to erase.
Thanks to God's mercy, this is possible.
What keeps me from erasing my past
in the sacrament of Reconciliation?

Create a pure heart in me, O God,
and put a new and loyal spirit in me. . . .
Give me again the joy that comes
from your salvation, and make me willing
to obey you.
PSALM 51:10, 12

WEEK 11
Day 5

You have been set free from sin.
ROMANS 6:22

A soldier in Indonesia bought a monkey
for a pet. Soon he noticed the monkey was
sensitive around the waist. Taking a look,
he found a raised welt around the monkey's
midsection. Pulling back the hair from the
welt, he saw the problem. When the
monkey was a baby, someone tied wire
around its middle and never took it off.
The wire was now embedded in the
monkey's flesh. That evening the soldier
shaved the hair around the wire and
carefully removed it. All the while, the
monkey lay there with amazing patience,
blinking its eyes. As soon as the operation
was over, the monkey jumped up and
down, leaped on the soldier, and hugged
him tightly.

The pain of confessing sin is nothing
compared to the pain
of being held bound by it.
Can I recall a time when God freed me
from some sin that held me bound
and in pain? To what extent
was my reaction like the monkey's?

Sins cannot be undone, only forgiven.
IGOR STRAVINSKY

When I did not confess my sins,
I was worn out from crying. . . .
Then I confessed my sins to you;
I did not conceal my wrongdoings. . . .
You forgave all my sins.

PSALM 32:3, 5

Years ago *This Week* magazine carried a moving story about a seventeen-year-old Dutch boy. He was a prisoner who had escaped from a Nazi camp during World War II. He was caught and sentenced to death. Shortly afterward, he wrote to his father: "Read this letter alone, and then tell Mother carefully. . . . In a little while at five o'clock it is going to happen . . . one moment, and then I shall be with God. . . . Is that, after all, such a dreadful transition? . . . I feel so strongly my nearness to God. I am fully prepared to die. . . . I have confessed all my sins . . . and have become very quiet.
[Signed] Klees"

Blessed is the person who will be able to say at death what Klees said. If I died right now, could I say what he did?

Those who forgive most
shall be most forgiven.

ENGLISH PROVERB

WEEK 11
Day 7 _____

*You have taken away my sorrow
and surrounded me with joy.*
PSALM 30:11

British violinist Peter Cropper was invited
to Finland for a special concert. As a
personal favor, the Royal Academy of
Music lent Peter their priceless 285-year-
old Stradivarius violin. That violin was
known the world over for its incredible
sound. At the concert, a nightmare
happened. Going on stage, Peter tripped
and fell. The violin broke into several
pieces. Peter flew home to England in a
state of shock. A master craftsperson,
Charles Beare, spent endless hours
repairing the violin. Then came the moment
of truth. What would the violin sound
like? Those present couldn't believe their
ears. The violin's sound was better than
before.

The story of that violin is my story.
Sin nearly destroyed me; but God,
the master craftsperson, repaired me.
My sound is now more beautiful than
it was before. What ought I to give God
in return for what God has given me?

True repentance is to cease to sin.
SAINT AMBROSE

WEEKLY MEETING
Sharing Agenda

1 What impact did the insertion of my name in the passage from Hosea have on my meditation?

2 Do I know someone who is messed up but who has a treasure inside? How might I help this person bring it forth?

3 When did someone put me down in front of friends? How would I advise a son or a daughter to handle such a situation in a Christlike way?

4 How eagerly and often do I turn to the sacrament of Reconciliation to "untattoo" the past?

5 To what extent do I experience the sacrament of Reconciliation as a loving encounter with a forgiving God?

6 When did I experience a quiet peace, such as Klees did?

7 What is one way the experience of having sinned and been forgiven made "my sound more beautiful"?

12 How grateful am I for God's forgiveness of me?

Daddy Long Legs is the story of an orphan girl who receives gifts from an unknown person. She grows through childhood and her teen years blessed with opportunities provided by her secret "parent." She tries to imagine what this wonderful person is like.

Then one day she discovers the identity of her benefactor. Her joy overflows! And as you share her excitement, you think, "How sad it would have been for her to go through life without having met or thanked this gracious person."

The story of *Daddy Long Legs* is a parable of God and each one of us. God gave us the gift of life, and God continues to give us gift upon gift. How sad it would be for us to go through life without having met or thanked our Benefactor.

This week's meditations focus on gratitude to God. The grace you ask before each meditation is beautifully expressed in these words by George Herbert:

O Thou who has given me so much, mercifully grant me one thing more— a grateful heart.   (slightly adapted)

Weekly Instruction

During this week, recite the concluding
prayer of each meditation ("Our Father
. . .") in an audible whisper. Pause after
each phrase or thought to let its meaning
sink in. Give special attention to these
words of the prayer:

Forgive us our trespasses
as we forgive those
who trespass against us.

Daily Reading

Karl Barth compared reading the Bible to
looking out the window of a tall building
down to a crowd of people on the street.
They are staring up at something hidden
from our view on the roof.

Developing the image, Frederick Buechner
compares interpreting the Bible to trying
to read the faces of the crowd and, through
them—with the help of the Holy Spirit—
discover what they see.

1	Where are the others	Lk 17:11–19
2	Give thanks to God	Col 3:12–17
3	Rejoice in the Lord	1 Thes 5:16–28
4	Proclaim God's glory	Ps 69:30–34
5	The Lord helped me	Ps 30:4–12
6	I thank God for you	Col 1:3–14
7	Sing to the Lord	Ps 100

WEEK 12
Day 1 _____

[Jesus told ten lepers,]
"Go and let the priests examine you."
On the way they were made clean. . . .
[Only one came back]
to give thanks to God.

LUKE 17:14, 18

In his book *Who Needs God?* Harold
Kushner tells about a man who disciplined
himself to write "thank you" in the lower
left-hand corner of the checks he wrote to
pay his bills. He wrote it on his checks to
the grocer, the phone company, the gas
company, the electric company—even on
his checks to the IRS. He didn't do this
because he thought these companies would
be impressed. He knew better than that.
He did it simply as his personal way of
reminding himself to be grateful for living
in a free country and for all the services
this freedom brought.

What system do I have to keep myself
from taking for granted the blessings
that God and others bestow on me daily?
What system might I devise for this?

Unexpressed gratitude
is like winking at someone in the dark.
You know how you feel about them,
but they don't.   ANONYMOUS

Sing to God
with thanksgiving in your hearts.
COLOSSIANS 3:16

Marathon runner Bill Rodgers was a
conscientious objector to the Vietnam
War. He was assigned to alternative
service in a home for retarded men. One
of those special men was named Joe. He
had the ability to focus on the good in life
and be grateful for it. Bill says: "Whenever
I saw Joe, he seemed to be wearing
a big welcome-to-my-world smile.
When I glimpsed him
at therapy sessions or workshops,
he was participating wholeheartedly,
eager to learn and grow. . . .
The smallest act of kindness . . .
made him brim with gratitude.
Joe found reasons to be grateful
even in the most trying circumstances."

How well do I keep my focus on the good
in life rather than on the bad?
How might I improve in this area?

Some complain
that God put thorns on roses;
others give thanks
that God put roses among thorns.
ANONYMOUS

WEEK 12
Day 3 _____

Be thankful in all circumstances.
1 THESSALONIANS 5:18

Corrie ten Boom and her sister Betsie
were put behind barbed wire during
World War II for helping Dutch Jews. One
day they were moved to a shelter completely
infested with fleas. Corrie became
depressed, but Betsie recalled a passage
from Saint Paul: "Be thankful in all
circumstances." So they knelt down and
thanked God for their new shelter, fleas
and all. In the weeks ahead, they enjoyed
a remarkable lack of supervision from the
guards. They were able to talk freely—
even read and discuss the Bible with other
prisoners. One day Corrie learned why.
Someone called the guards to come in and
settle a dispute. They refused, saying,
"You settle it. We're not entering that flea
bag." Now Corrie understood why the
prisoners enjoyed so much freedom. And
her mind went back to the day when she
and Betsie gave thanks for their shelter,
fleas and all.

Can I recall a time when an apparent cross
turned out to be a great blessing?

Gratitude is a sign of noble souls.
AESOP

*I will proclaim [God's] greatness
by giving [God] thanks.*

PSALM 69:30

Mention Bugs Bunny and people smile.
Mention Charlie Jones and people frown.
But Bugs Bunny owes his popularity to
Charlie Jones. In the 1930s, Jones was a
struggling artist in Warner Brothers
Studio. He took over the Bugs Bunny
project and developed it into one of
Hollywood's best-loved cartoons. About
the same time, Walt Disney created the
famous "Three Little Pigs" cartoon. Jones
wrote Disney a letter of congratulations.
Disney was so grateful that he wrote a
thank-you note back. Years later, Disney
lay dying in a hospital; Charlie visited
him. During the visit, Disney recalled the
letter Jones had written him thirty years
earlier. He thanked him again. "I treasure
your letter," he told Jones. "You're the
only animator who ever wrote to me."

When was the last time I congratulated
or thanked a colleague or associate?

*God has two dwellings.
One is in heaven;
the other in a meek and thankful heart.*

IZAAK WALTON

WEEK 12
Day 5 _____

Sing praise to the LORD,
all . . . faithful people!
Remember what the Holy One has done,
and give . . . thanks!

PSALM 30:4

A teacher asked her students, "Which is more important—the sun or the moon?" "The moon!" said little Mary. "Why do you say that?" asked the teacher. "Well," said Mary, "the moon gives us light at night when we really *need* it, while the sun gives us light during the day, when we really *don't* need it." After thinking about Mary's response for a minute, we realize that her attitude toward the sun mirrors our attitude toward God. Mary took daylight for granted, forgetting that it came from the sun. In a similar way, we take the gift of life for granted, forgetting that it comes from God.

What is one thing God has given me— or one thing God has not given me— that I have taken for granted and forget to give thanks for?

When every bone in our body aches,
we can, at least, thank God
that we're not a herring.

QUIN RYAN (adapted)

In the name of our Lord Jesus Christ,
always give thanks for everything
to God the Father.

EPHESIANS 5:20

Henry Ward Beecher says: "Imagine
someone gave you a dish of sand mixed
with fine iron filings. Imagine you search
for the filings with your eyes and comb
for them with your fingers. But you can't
find them. Now imagine that you take a
tiny magnet and draw it through the sand.
It comes out covered with iron filings."
Beecher concludes: "Ungrateful people are
like your fingers combing the sand. They
find little in life to be thankful for.
Grateful people are like the magnet
sweeping through the sand. They find
hundreds of things."

If God asked me to isolate the three things
I am most grateful for in my life, what
would they be? Why these?

For the flowers
that bloom about our feet;
For tender grass so fresh and sweet;
For song of bird and hum of bee;
For all things we hear and see,
Father in heaven, we thank thee.

RALPH WALDO EMERSON

WEEK 12
Day 7 _____

*I thank you, L*ORD*, with all my heart. . . .*
*L*ORD*, your love is eternal.*
Complete the work that you have begun.

PSALM 138:1, 8

This meditation ends the "First Week"
of *The Spiritual Exercises of Saint Ignatius.*
During this First Week you have evaluated
how well you are living your life according
to the purpose for which God created you.
Saint Ignatius presents his "spiritual
exercises" in such a way that you can stop
at this point or go on to the "Second
Week." The Second Week focuses on how
Jesus lived his life according to the
purpose for which he was sent into the
world. In the words of the Broadway
musical *Godspell,* the Second Week invites
you to get to know Jesus more *clearly* so
that you may love him more *dearly* and
follow him more *nearly.*

Do I feel that God is calling me to stop
at this point, go on to the Second Week,
or take a few weeks off and then decide
what God is calling me to do?

Doing the best thing at this moment
puts you in the best place
for the next moment.

OPRAH WINFREY

WEEKLY MEETING
_____ Sharing Agenda

1   What system do I have to keep myself from taking for granted the blessings that God and others bestow on me daily? What system might I devise for this?

2   How well do I keep my focus on the good in life rather than on the bad? What system might I devise to do this better?

3   Can I recall a time when a cross in my life turned out to be a blessing in disguise?

4   When was the last time I complimented or congratulated a colleague or associate? What keeps me from doing this more often?

5   What is one thing that God has given me—or not given me—that I have taken for granted and for which I should give thanks?

6   For what three things in my life am I most grateful? Why these?

7   Do I feel that God is calling me to stop at this point, go on to the "Second Week," or take a few weeks off and then decide what God is calling me to do?

II
DECISION

The "Second Week" of
The Spiritual Exercises of Saint Ignatius
focuses on this great mystery:
The second person of the Trinity,
in the person of Jesus,
took flesh and lived among us.

This incredible mystery inspires us
to pray with Saint Richard of Chichester
the words that inspired the song
in the musical *Godspell*:

Lord, of thee three things I pray:
To see thee more clearly,
Love thee more dearly,
Follow thee more nearly,
Day by day.

133

13 Why did Jesus live among us?
(Incarnation)

Mark Twain wrote a story called "The Terrible Catastrophe." It concerns a group of people who get trapped in a terrible situation. They are doomed to die. There is no way they can escape.

Mark Twain didn't want the story to end unhappily, but he didn't see how he could save the people. So he concluded his story with these two sentences: "I have these characters in such a fix that even I can't get them out of it. Anyone who thinks he can is welcome to try."

Two thousand years ago, the human race was trapped like Twain's characters. Sin had entered the world and was spreading out of control. God saw the situation and didn't want it to end tragically. God loved us too much for that. So the second person of the Trinity came among us to save us.

It is this great mystery that you ponder this week. The grace you ask for is this:

Lord, of thee three things I pray:
To see thee more clearly,
Love thee more dearly,
Follow thee more nearly.

Weekly Instruction

The first step in God's plan was to pick someone to be Jesus' mother. God chose the Virgin Mary.

In Mary's honor you might end each meditation this week with the "Hail Holy Queen." Columbus's sailors gathered on the deck of their ship each night at sunset to sing it. It reads:

Hail Holy Queen, mother of mercy,
our life, our sweetness, our hope.
To you we cry,
poor banished children of Eve.
To you we direct our sighs, mourning
and weeping in this valley of tears.
Be merciful to us,
loving advocate, Virgin Mary,
and after this our exile,
show us your son, Jesus.

Daily Reading

1 God chooses Mary   Lk 1:26-38
2 Mary carries Jesus   Lk 1:39-45
3 Jesus comes among us   Jn 1:1-14
4 Jesus is our shepherd   Jn 10:1-10
5 Jesus is God's Son   Heb 1:1-3
6 Jesus is our light   Mt 4:12-16
7 Jesus left an example   1 Pt 2:21-25

WEEK 13
Day 1 _____

*[God sent an angel to Nazareth
to a girl named Mary.] The angel said . . .
"You will become pregnant and give birth
to a son, and you will name him Jesus."*

LUKE 1:30-31

A college student wrote: "Today
I saw a water lily growing in a pond.
It had the purest yellow I'd ever seen.
The lily—a precious treasure—
was unconcerned about whether
anyone noticed its astounding beauty.
As I sat there,
watching it unfold its petals noiselessly,
I thought of Mary pregnant with Jesus.
She, too, was a precious treasure.
She, too, was unconcerned about whether
anyone noticed her astounding beauty.
But to those who did, she shared a secret.
Her beauty came not from her, but from
the Jesus life unfolding its petals
noiselessly within her."

If I were God, what would I look for
in the one who would parent my Son?

*Welcome all wonders in one sight!
Eternity shut in a span!
Summer in Winter, Day in Night!
Heaven in earth and God in man!*

RICHARD CRASHAW

*[Emperor Augustus ordered the people
to return to their birthplace to register
for a census. Joseph went to Bethlehem
with Mary, where she] gave birth to
her first son, wrapped him in cloths and
laid him in a manger—there was no room
for them to stay in the inn.*

LUKE 2:7

Author Morton Kelsey writes:
"I am very glad that the divine child
was born in a stable, because my soul
is very much like a stable,
filled with strange unsatisfied longings,
with guilt and animial-like impulses. . . .
If the holy One could be born
in such a place,
the holy One can be born in me also.
I am not excluded."

Do I have any special reason
for being "glad that the divine child
was born in a stable"?
Why would God pick such a birthplace?

*Christmas is a good time
to get a little crazy.
After all, God did.
God became a human being.
That's pretty crazy.*

JIM AUER

WEEK 13
Day 3 _____

We write to you about the Word of life,
which has existed from the very beginning.
We have heard it . . . seen it . . .
and our hands have touched it.

1 JOHN 1:1

In his poem "A Kind of Prayer," Cyril
Egan describes a person searching
frantically for something. The person
looks high and low. One day a friend asks,
"Tell me! What are you looking for?"
The person replies, "I'm looking for God."
Then the person adds quickly:
"Don't tell me I'll find him in my heart
(Though in a sense that's true);
And don't tell me I'll find him
in my fellow man
(Though in a sense that's true, too).
What I'm looking for is a God making
a five-sense breakthrough to humanity."
The God for whom the person was looking
entered human history 2,000 years ago in
the town of Bethlehem.

What are some reasons why I am glad
that God made a "five-sense breakthrough"
into human history?

What we need is people who know God
other than by hearsay.

THOMAS CARLYLE (slightly adapted)

Of his own free will he gave up all . . .
and appeared in human likeness.

PHILLIPIANS 2:7

A woman was seated by a fireplace,
thinking about Christmas. The whole
thing seemed absurd. Why would God
take flesh and live among us? Then she
heard a noise outdoors. She saw a dozen
geese groping about in the snow—cold and
confused. She went outside and tried to
herd them into her warm garage. But the
more she tried to help them, the more they
scattered across the lawn. Finally she
gave up. Then an odd thought came to
her: "If just for a minute I could become
a goose and talk to them in their language,
I could explain that what I was trying to
do was for their happiness." Then it
struck her. That's what Christmas is all
about! It's about God becoming a human
to teach us what is for our happiness.

What one thing Jesus taught is for our
happiness do I sometimes question? Why?

A Christmas candle is a lovely thing;
It makes no noise at all,
But softly gives itself away;
While quite unselfish, it grows small.

EVA K. LOGUE

*[Jesus] reflects
the brightness of God's glory.*
HEBREWS 1:3

A *Peanuts* cartoon shows Linus saying to
Charlie Brown, "That's ridiculous!"
Charlie replies, "Maybe so! But come and
see for yourself." They go into the living
room where Snoopy is sitting on the TV
set. His ears are pointed up and out like
an antenna. Charlie says, "See! It does
make the picture better." An amazed
Linus says to Charlie, "You're right!" A
college girl said of this cartoon, "If Jesus
were living today, he might use it as a
parable to clarify his relationship to the
Father." Her point is this: As Snoopy gave
Charlie and Linus a clearer image on the
TV screen, so Jesus gives us a clearer
image of God. The Scriptures express it
this way:

"[Jesus] reflects the brightness
of God's glory and is the exact likeness
of God's own being" (HEBREWS 1:3).

In what one way, especially, does Jesus
give me a clearer image of God?

*He wakes desires you never may forget;
He shows you stars you never saw before.*
ALFRED LORD TENNYSON

"I am the light of the world. . . .
Whoever follows me
will have the light of life
and will never walk in darkness."

JOHN 8:12

The book *Night Flight* deals with the early years of aviation. It describes the adventures of aviators who used to fly at night, without radar or radio. The book is not only a gripping story about the early years of aviation but also an instructive parable about the human situation before Jesus' coming. Life was a mystery. We didn't know where we came from or where we were going. We were like night fliers lost in darkness and fog. Then Jesus came into the world. Jesus did not take away the fog and the night. He did something more incredible. He got into the plane with us. We are no longer flying blind through night and fog. We have a copilot sitting beside us.

How frequently and concerning what, especially, do I consult my copilot sitting beside me?

Sun of my soul! Thou Savior dear,
It is not night if Thou be near.

JOHN KEBLE

WEEK 13
Day 7 _____

[Christ] left you an example . . .
that you would follow in his steps.
1 PETER 2:21

A prince had a crooked back that kept him
from being the kind of prince he wanted
to be. One day the king had a sculptor
make a statue that portrayed the prince
with a straight back. He placed it in the
garden. When the prince saw it, he
meditated on it and desired to be like it.
Soon people began to say, "The prince's
back is getting straighter." When the
prince heard this, he began to spend hours
meditating on the statue. Then one day
he stood as straight as the statue. That
story is a parable of you and me. We too
were born to be a princess or a prince, but
a defect kept us from being what we were
meant to be. Then God sent Jesus to show
us how we can become what we were
meant to be.

What do the king, the prince, the prince's
crooked back, the statue, and studying the
statue stand for in the parable? What does
the parable say to me?

By a Carpenter we were made, and only by
that Carpenter can we be remade.
DESIDERIUS ERASMUS

WEEKLY MEETING
Sharing Agenda

1 If I were God, what would I look for in the one to parent my Son? Why this?

2 What might have been some reasons why Jesus was born where he was?

3 What are some of the reasons why I am glad that God made a "five-sense breakthrough" into history?

4 What one thing that Jesus taught is for our happiness do I have trouble dealing with?

5 In what way, especially, has Jesus given me a clearer image of God?

6 Of the four steps in the prayer process (read, think, speak, listen), which do I find most satisfying when I communicate with Jesus? Why?

7 What struck me most in the parable of the prince with the crooked back? What might it be saying to me?

14 How did Jesus differ from other leaders?
(Call of the King)

The novel *The Apostle* takes place in Rome in the early days of Christianity. It describes a large group of Christians imprisoned in a dark dungeon. They are to remain there indefinitely, until they will be hauled up through a ceiling door to be executed for their faith. The mood is one of deep sadness.

One day the ceiling door opens, and a shaft of light pierces the darkness as another Christian is lowered to await execution. Amazingly, he is singing at the top of his voice. "Who is this man?" everyone asks. Then word spreads rapidly. "It is the apostle Paul."

Paul's joyful presence is so contagious that soon everyone starts singing. In seconds, the dungeon is changed from a place of sadness to one of joy.
It is this kind of change that the presence of Jesus had on our world.

This week's meditations focus on the presence and the leadership of Jesus in our world. Specifically, they focus on the invitation Jesus makes to us to join him in the work of building up God's Kingdom in our world. The grace you ask for is:

Lord, give to my ears the sensitivity
to hear the voice of Jesus,
and give to my heart the generosity
to do whatever Jesus asks of me.

Weekly Instruction

One way spiritual directors suggest you place yourself in God's presence is to focus on your breathing. Breathing points to God's presence inside you. For example, Scripture portrays God as breathing into us the breath of life (GENESIS 2:7).

Therefore, each day this week, before beginning your meditation, close your eyes and monitor your breathing for a period of fifteen exhalations. At the end of the week, decide whether this helped you place yourself in God's presence. If it helped, you may wish to continue it.

Daily Reading

1 Jesus' attitude   Phil 2:5–11
2 Jesus' style   Mk 10:35–45
3 Jesus' magnetism   Jn 7:32–46
4 Jesus' revelation   Jn 14:1–14
5 Jesus' charge   Jn 15:1–10
6 Jesus' impact   Jn 12:12–19
7 Jesus' invitation   Lk 9:23–27

✘ WEEK 14
Day 1

*[Jesus] was humble and walked the path
of obedience—all the way to death.*

PHILIPPIANS 2:8

"Here is a young man who was born . . .
of a peasant woman. . . . He worked in
a carpenter shop until he was thirty. . . .
He never owned a home. He never had
a family. He never went to college. . . .
He had no credentials but himself.
While he was still a young man, the tide
of public opinion turned against him.
His friends ran away. . . . He was nailed
to a cross between two thieves. . . .
When he was dead, he was laid
in a borrowed grave. . . .
Nineteen centuries have come and gone,
and today he is . . . the leader of the column
of progress. I am far within the mark
when I say that all the armies that ever
marched, and all the kings who ever
reigned, put together, have not affected
the life of man upon this earth as has that
One Solitary Life."

AUTHOR UNKNOWN

✘ How do I explain Jesus' impact on history?

*People want to know how much you care
before they care how much you know.*

JAMES E HIND

*[Jesus said,] "The Son of Man did not come
to be served; he came to serve."*

MARK 10:45

"The Watermelon Hunter" is an Islamic
parable about a traveler who strayed into
the "Land of the Fools." Outside a village,
he saw people fleeing in terror from a field.
They were shouting hysterically, "A
monster is in our field!" The traveler drew
nearer and saw the monster was only a
watermelon, something the fools had
never seen. To show how fearless he was,
the traveler sliced up the melon and ate
it. When the people saw this, they grew
even more hysterical, shouting, "He's
worse than the monster!" Months later
another traveler strayed into the "Land
of the Fools," and the same scene repeated
itself. This time the traveler didn't play
the hero. Instead, he took up residence
among the fools and taught them about
watermelons. They eventually cultivated
and ate them.

How does this story mirror a difference
between Jesus and many other leaders?

*[Jesus said,] "Learn from me,
because I am gentle and humble in spirit."*

MATTHEW 11:29

[Even Jesus' opponents said,] *"Nobody has ever talked the way this man does!"*

JOHN 7:46

H. G. Wells was asked to pick history's greatest leader. Although he was not a Christian, Wells picked Jesus. He said he realized that many people believe Jesus is divine, but a historian must disregard this fact. He has to stick to uncontested facts. Wells picked Jesus because of two great ideas Jesus released: the Fatherhood of God (all have a common origin) and the Kingdom of God (all have a common destiny). Wells said these ideas sparked "one of the most revolutionary changes of . . . human thought. . . . The historian's test of an individual's greatness is 'What did he leave to grow?' Did he start men to thinking along fresh lines with a vigor that persisted after him? By this test Jesus stands first."

What challenge does Jesus pose for me?

Be a disciple!
Care more than others think necessary.
Trust more than others think wise.
Serve more than others think practical.
Expect more than others think possible.

ANONYMOUS

"I am the way, the truth, and the life."
JOHN 14:6

Napoleon and General Bertrand were
discussing Jesus. Bertrand said Jesus was
just a great human leader. Napoleon
disagreed, saying: "I know men, and I tell
you Jesus Christ is not a man. . . . I have
so inspired multitudes that they would die
for me. . . . A word from me, then the
sacred fire was kindled in their hearts.
I do, indeed, possess the secret of this
magical power that lifts the soul, but I
could never impart it to anyone. None of
my generals ever learned it from me; nor
have I the means of perpetuating . . . love
for me in the hearts of men." Napoleon's
point is a good one. Other leaders can only
excite us. They cannot reach inside
themselves and take a part of their own
spirit and then place it inside us. Jesus
can. And this is where Jesus differs from
all other human leaders.

What part of Jesus' spirit should I seek?

*It is Christ in you that lives your life,
that helps the poor, that tells the truth,
that fights the battle, and
that wins the crown.*

PHILLIPS BROOKS

WEEK 14
Day 5

[Jesus said,]
"I am the vine, and you are the branches.
Whoever remains in me, and I in him,
will bear much fruit."

JOHN 15:5

Jesus is uniquely different from all other
human leaders. Other leaders can impact
us only psychologically. That is, they can
inspire us. Jesus can impact us not only
psychologically but also mystically. What
does this mean? It means that other
leaders can only inflame our emotions and
excite our imagination. They cannot
transfuse us with their own personal
spirit, power, and strength. This is precisely
what Jesus can do. Jesus can put his spirit
inside us. He can share his power with
us. He can enter our minds and our hearts
and help us become what we could never
become alone.

How might I open myself more fully
to Jesus' transforming power and spirit?

"Listen! I stand at the door and knock;
if anyone hears my voice and opens
the door, I will come into his house
and eat with him,
and he will eat with me."

REVELATION 3:20

*"Wherever you go, I will go;
wherever you live, I will live."*
RUTH 1:16

Imagine the following. A dynamic leader
emerges in our world. The leader's charism
cuts across all national and social
boundaries. Everyone trusts this person
and recognizes that the "hand of God"
rests upon this person. Now imagine this
leader gives a speech. With compassion
and understanding, the leader spells out
programs for curbing corruption, reducing
drug traffic and crime, revitalizing ghetto
areas, reforming the prison system, erasing
poverty. Even the most realistic politicians
are impressed by the leader's grasp of
the problems and insights for dealing
with them. The leader ends the address
by asking for volunteers at every level
and in every area of the proposed
programs.

What might keep me from volunteering?
What would motivate me to volunteer?

*You see things as they are;
and you ask "Why?"
But I dream things that never were;
and I ask "Why not?"*
GEORGE BERNARD SHAW

WEEK 14
Day 7 _____

"If anyone wants to come with me,
he must forget himself . . .
and follow me." LUKE 9:23

Alan Paton has an inspiring conversation
in *Oh, But Your Land Is Beautiful.* It's
between a black person and a white
person. Both have put their lives on the
line for racial justice in South Africa.
When one of them observes that they may
end up with a lot of body scars, the other
says: "Well, look at it this way. When I
get there, the great Judge will say, 'Where
are your scars?' And if I haven't any, he
will ask, 'Were there no causes worthy of
getting scars?' "

What is one scar from one worthy cause
that the "great judge" will see on me
when I "get there"?

Far better is it
to dare mighty things,
to win glorious triumphs,
even though checkered by failures,
than to rank with those poor spirits
who neither enjoy much nor suffer much
because they live in the gray twilight
that knows neither victory nor defeat.
THEODORE ROOSEVELT

WEEKLY MEETING
Sharing Agenda

1 Apart from the fact that I believe Jesus to be the Son of God, how do I explain the positive impact that Jesus has had on history?

2 How does "The Watermelon Hunter" illustrate one difference between Jesus and many other leaders?

3 What is there about Jesus that motivates me to "care more than others think necessary" or "expect more than others think possible"?

4 What is one portion of his "spirit" that I would like Jesus to place inside me? Why this?

5 What is one thing I might do to open myself more fully to Jesus' transforming spirit and power?

6 How free am I to volunteer for whatever role the "dynamic leader" might wish me to play in the proposed programs?

7 What is one scar from one worthy cause that Jesus will see on me when I stand before him on the last day? Why don't I have more scars?

15 Why did Jesus embrace the lifestyle he did?
(Two Standards)

On a trip to the Holy Land, James Martin bought a tiny nativity set. When he arrived at the Tel Aviv airport to return home, security was tight. Officials x-rayed each tiny figure in his set, even the infant Jesus. They explained, "We must be sure there's nothing explosive hidden in the set."

Afterward Martin thought, "If those officials only knew the explosive power hidden in that set!" Martin was referring to its "message"—that the Son of God chose to take a human nature, be born in a stable, and live among us as—

- a *poor person* ("Birds have nests, but the Son of Man has no place" |LUKE 9:58|),
- a *dishonored person* ("The Son of Man . . . must . . . be rejected" |LUKE 17:24-25|),
- a *humble person* ("Learn from me . . . I am gentle and humble" |MATTHEW 11:29|).

The surprising *lifestyle* Jesus chose differs totally from the one the devil uses to tempt people. For example, on one occasion the devil made this offer: "I will give you all this power and all this wealth" (LUKE 4:6).

This week's meditations focus on the lifestyle of Jesus—and why he chose it—in contrast to the lifestyle the devil proposes to people. The grace you ask for is:

Lord, help me understand why the devil proposes a lifestyle of attachment, and help me appreciate why Jesus chose a lifestyle of detachment.

Weekly Instruction

Behind the lifestyle the devil proposes is a *strategy of attachment* (to wealth, honors, and vain pride). Satan's goal is to *enslave people* by having them become attached to worldly things rather than heavenly things. Jesus' lifestyle is the opposite. Behind it is a *strategy of detachment* (from wealth, honors, and vain pride). Jesus' goal is to *free people* from attachment to worldly things so they can pursue heavenly things.

Daily Reading

1	Riches in heaven	Mt 6:19-21
2	You are an obstacle	Mt 16:21-27
3	Would-be followers	Lk 9:57-62
4	Hearts and treasures	Lk 12:22-34
5	Whose friend am I	Jas 4:4-10
6	Come up, my friend	Lk 14:7-14
7	Take your choice	Lk 16:13-15

WEEK 15
Day 1 _____

*[Jesus prayed to the Father
for his disciples,]
"I do not ask you to take them
out of the world, but I do ask you
to keep them safe from the Evil One."*
JOHN 17:15

The famous Chicago fire took place on
October 8, 1871, killing over 300 people.
That same night, the logging town of
Peshtigo, Wisconsin, burned down, killing
over 1,300 people. News of the Peshtigo
fire, however, did not reach the public
immediately, because the telegraph lines
burned. Columnist L. M. Boyd says:
"When the Peshtigo news finally came
through, the papers were so absorbed with
the Chicago fire there was little room for
the holocaust, which had taken more than
four times as many lives." The story of
the two fires illustrates that worldly
judgments are not always objective or fair.

To what extent am I more concerned
about the world's judgment than God's?

*On Judgment Day
we will all receive our just due.
People honored by the world
may rank last; while people dishonored
by the world may rank first.*

[Jesus said],
"I must . . . be put to death. . . ."
[Peter said,] "God forbid it, Lord!" . . .
Jesus turned around and said to Peter . . .
"You are an obstacle in my way,
because these thoughts of yours
don't come from God, but from man."

MATTHEW 16:21-23

On the last page of his book *The Magic Maker*, poet E. E. Cummings quotes from a letter he wrote to a high school editor. The editor had asked him about the pitfalls that lay in the way of someone interested in pursuing a career in poetry. Cummings described the biggest pitfall: "To be nobody but yourself in a world which is doing its best, night and day, to make you everybody else— it means to fight the hardest battle which any human being can fight, and never stop fighting."

How am I fighting the battle that Cummings referred to in his letter— to be the person God made me to be, and not the one the world wants me to be?

We forfeit three-fourths of ourselves
to be like other people.

ARTHUR SCHOPENHAUER

WEEK 15
Day 3

A man said to Jesus, "I will follow you wherever you go." Jesus said to him, "Foxes have holes, and birds have nests," but the Son of Man has no place to lie."

LUKE 9:57-58

Rudyard Kipling won the Nobel Prize for literature. His short story "The Man Who Would Be King" is one of the finest stories ever written. His poem "If" is still memorized by many. And the movie of his novel *Jungle Book* enjoys frequent reruns on television. One of Kipling's memorable speeches was a commencement address at McGill University in Montreal. Warning the graduates against overconcern for worldly honors and wealth, he said, "Someday you will meet a person who cares for none of these things. Then you will know how really poor you are."

What are some concrete indications that I am far more concerned about honors and wealth than Jesus would be today?

It's good to have money and the things that money can buy, but it's good, too, to check once in a while and make sure you haven't lost the things money can't buy.

GEORGE HORACE LORIMER

*[Jesus said,] "Your heart will always be
where your riches are."*   LUKE 12:34

Former football great O.J. Simpson wrote:
"I sit in my house in Buffalo and sometimes
I get so lonely it's unbelievable. Life has
been so good to me. I've got a great wife,
good kids, money, my own health—I'm
lonely and bored. . . . I often wonder why
so many rich people commit suicide.
Money sure isn't a cure-all." Similarly,
after fire destroyed Kareem Abdul-
Jabbar's plush home, the former Los
Angeles Lakers star said: "My whole
perspective changed after the fire. I think
it's more important now for me to spend
time with my son Amir and appreciate
other things besides basketball. There
are a lot of things that are more
important."

What is my "philosophy" concerning
worldly honors and possessions? Why?

*Riches are the least worthy things
that God can give a person.
What are they . . . compared
to skill, wisdom, and understanding?
Yet we toil for them day and night.*
    MARTIN LUTHER

WEEK 15
Day 5 _____

*"God resists the proud,
but gives grace to the humble. . . ."
Humble yourselves before the Lord,
and [the Lord] will lift you up.*

JAMES 4:6, 10

Charles Colson was a top Nixon aide who
went to prison in the Watergate scandal.
He has since undergone a religious
conversion and works full time preaching
the Gospel, especially in prisons and on
college campuses. Colson was deeply
influenced by this passage from C. S.
Lewis's book *Mere Christianity:*
"Pride leads to every other vice: it is
the complete anti-God state of mind. . . .
As long as you are proud
you cannot know God. A proud man
is always looking down on things. . . .
As long as you are looking down,
you cannot see something
that is above you."

How big is the problem of pride—and its
companion, envy—in my life? Examples?

*There is no greater pride than in seeking
to humiliate ourselves beyond measure!
And sometimes there's no truer humility
than to attempt great things for God.*

ABBE DE SAINT-CYRAN

[Jesus said,]
"Everyone who makes himself great
will be humbled,
and everyone who humbles himself
will be made great."

LUKE 14:11

The cartoon character Charlie Brown is based on a real person. He worked with juvenile delinquents, often housing them temporarily in his own home. After the real Charlie Brown died in 1983, a friend said of him, "He saw his own life as the doing of daily works of charity in imitation of Christ and the saints." Charles Schulz— the Charlie Brown cartoonist—was a friend of the real Charlie. He sometimes offered Charlie a share in the profits from some cartoon spinoffs, like T-shirts. But Charlie refused. He had no big interest in money. Nor did Charlie go about telling people that he was the real Charlie Brown.

Can I ever recall bragging about myself or seeking recognition from others? To what extent do I still do it? Why?

Until we lose ourselves
there is no hope of finding ourselves.

HENRY MILLER

WEEK 15
Day 7

*[Jesus said,] "No servant
can be the slave of two masters."*
LUKE 16:13

The film *Rosemary's Baby* portrays Satan
being born into our world. Suppose Satan
was actually born into our world. How
would we be tempted to follow Satan?
Saint Ignatius gives a reply in his
meditation "The Two Standards." First,
Satan would lead us from a noble striving
for security to a wrongful stockpiling of
possessions *(wealth)*. Second, Satan would
lead us from a noble striving for acceptance
to a wrongful striving for recognition
(honor). Finally, Satan would lead us from
a noble appreciation of our self-worth to
a wrongful indulgence in self-love *(pride)*.
Jesus' strategy is to protect us from
Satan's strategy. Jesus invites us to
imitate him and to distance ourselves
from wealth, honor, and pride.

Whose lifestyle and strategy—Jesus' or
Satan's—am I currently being most
influenced by? How do I feel about this?

*It is so stupid of modern civilization
to have given up believing in the devil
when [the devil] is the only explanation
of it.*
RONALD KNOX

WEEKLY MEETING
Sharing Agenda

1 What is one area of my life where I am currently tempted to be more concerned about the world's judgment than God's judgment?

2 Where I am currently experiencing a pressure to be the person the world wants me to be rather than the one God wants me to be?

3 What are some concrete indications that I am far more concerned about honors and possessions than Jesus would be if he were living today?

4 What is my "philosophy" concerning worldly honors and possessions?

5 How big is the problem of pride—and its companion, envy—in my life? Examples?

6 Can I ever recall bragging about myself or seeking recognition from others? Example? Why?

7 Whose lifestyle and strategy—Jesus' or Satan's—am I currently being most influenced by? How do I feel about this?

16 How free am I to follow Jesus?
(Three Classes of People)

In *Winning by Letting Go,* Elizabeth Brenner tells how people in rural India catch monkeys. First they cut a hole in a box. Then they put a tasty nut in the box. The hole is just big enough for the monkey to put its hand through. But once the monkey clutches the nut, its fist is too big to withdraw. So the monkey has two choices: release the nut and go free, or hold on to it and stay trapped. Monkeys often elect to hold on to the nut.

The monkey's situation is not unlike our situation when it comes to following Jesus. We want to follow Jesus more closely, but at the same time we find ourselves wanting to hold on to something that keeps us from doing so.

This week's meditations deal with this dilemma. Their purpose is to help you come to grips with whatever might be keeping you from following Jesus as you would like. The grace you ask before each meditation is:

Lord, help me let go of whatever is keeping me from following you.

Weekly Instruction

This week's meditations are especially important. You might consider seeking God's help by doing some special service for others or by making some special sacrifice, like not eating between meals.

During this week, make a special effort to record whatever feelings or insights that occur during each meditation. You need not record these at length. Two or three sentences are usually enough. For example, you may simply write:

Week 16: Day 1: *Lord, today you helped me see that one thing I need to try to "let go of" is worry. You also showed me that my worry stems more from a concern for what others may think of me rather than from what you may think of me. Thank you for this insight.*

Daily Reading

1	Rich young person	Mt 19:16–22
2	Loving service	Lk 17:7–10
3	Cost of discipleship	Lk 14:25–33
4	Unless the grain dies	Jn 12:20–24
5	Four kinds of seed	Lk 8:4–15
6	You clothed me	Mt 25:31–40
7	Excuses! Excuses!	Lk 14:15–24

WEEK 16
Day 1 _____

[Jesus said,]
"If your right eye causes you to sin,
take it out and throw it away!
It is much better for you
to lose a part of your body
than to have your whole body
thrown into hell."

MATTHEW 5:29

The medusa is a jellyfish that makes its
home in the Bay of Naples, off the Italian
coast. A nudibranch snail also makes its
home there. Occasionally, the jellyfish
swallows the snail. But then something
unusual happens. The snail's protective
shell keeps the jellyfish from digesting it.
At this point, the tiny snail turns the
tables on the jellyfish. It starts to eat the
jellyfish from the inside. Unless it is
expelled, the tiny snail will eventually
consume the jellyfish.

Is there a "snail" that I may have
ingested into my system and need to expel,
if I am to follow Jesus more closely and
live out his plan for me? What might it be,
and how might I expel it?

Those who know others are learned.
Those who know themselves are wise.

LAO-TSZE

[The LORD says,] "As high as the heavens are above the earth, so high are my ways and thoughts above yours."

ISAIAH 55:9

Bill Havens, a member of the four-man American canoe team, was scheduled to compete in the 1924 Olympics. Then the doctor told him that his wife would give birth to their baby sometime during the games. After pondering the situation, Bill decided his place was with his wife. And so, without fanfare, he withdrew from the canoe team. As it turned out, the team won the gold medal and Bill's wife was late in giving birth to a son, Frank. Bill could have competed and still returned in time for his son's birth. Years passed. In July 1952, a cable arrived for Bill. It was from Helsinki, where the Olympics were in progress. It read: "Dad, I won. I'm bringing home the gold medal you lost while waiting for me to be born."

Can I recall giving up something I had always dreamed of, because it conflicted with a duty to a loved one?

*Duty makes us do things well,
but love makes us do them beautifully.*

E. C. McKENZIE

WEEK 16
Day 3 _____

*[Jesus said,] "Whoever loses his life
for me and for the gospel will save it."*
MARK 8:35

George Burns made a film called *Oh, God!*
He played the part of God and wore thick
glasses and a funny little hat. John Denver
played a supermarket employee. One day
God appeared to the employee with a
message for the world. Getting people to
take the message seriously turned out to
be next to impossible. The employee found
himself on the verge of losing his job.
Exasperated, he turned to God and said,
"Preaching your word is costing me my
job!" God replied, "That's not a bad trade,
is it? Lose your job and save the world."
It's so easy to get lost in our own little
world and to see only our own problems.
It's so easy to think only of ourselves
and not to think of the greater good of
everyone.

To what extent am I prone to get lost
in my own little world and
let my little problems blind me
to the bigger ones of people around me?

*To ease another's heartbreak
is to forget one's own.*
MALCOLM MUGGERIDGE

*[A friend said to David,] "I will
always go with you wherever you go,
even if it means death."*

2 SAMUEL 15:21

For thirty years failure dogged Abraham
Lincoln. A list of his failures reads:
1832   was defeated for the legislature
1833   failed in business
1836   suffered a nervous breakdown
1843   lost the nomination for Congress
1854   was defeated for the Senate
1856   lost the vice presidential bid
When he was elected president in 1860,
Lincoln was prepared for the ordeal of the
Civil War years. Another man might have
collapsed under its trials. Not Lincoln. He
had learned to say yes to whatever God
had chosen for him: sickness over health,
poverty over wealth, dishonor over honor.
On Good Friday, 1865, Lincoln said yes
to the final choice: a short life over a long
one. He was assassinated.

How open am I to the option of saying yes
to the things Lincoln did,
if that is what God has chosen for me?

*To love is to know the sacrifices
which eternity exacts from life.*
JOHN OLIVER HOBBES

*[Jesus said,] "The seeds that fell
on rocky ground stand for those
who hear the message and receive it. . . .
But . . . when the time of testing comes,
they fall away."* LUKE 8:13

Two brothers, Clarence and Robert,
committed their lives to Jesus in their
youth. Clarence grew up and became a
civil rights activist. Working for these
rights was hard in the 1960s. Racial
tension was high. People staged sit-ins.
Police used dogs and fire hoses to disperse
them. Robert grew up and became a
lawyer. One day Clarence asked Robert
for legal help in a civil rights matter.
Robert refused, saying it could hurt his
political future. When Clarence asked him
about his commitment to Jesus, Robert
said, "I do follow Jesus, but I'm not going
to get crucified like he was." Clarence
said, "Robert, you're not a follower of
Jesus; you're only a fan."

In what way might I be more of a fan
of Jesus than a follower?

*The only thing necessary for the triumph
of evil is for good people to do nothing.*
EDMUND BURKE

WEEK 16
Day 6

*[Jesus said,] " 'I was . . . naked and you
clothed me. . . . Whenever you did this
for one of the least . . . you did it for me!"*

MATTHEW 25:35-36, 39

A king with no heirs invited qualified
young people to be interviewed, with a
view to succeeding him. A poverty-
stricken young man felt an inner call to
apply. He worked day and night to buy
provisions for the journey and clothes for
the interview. After weeks of travel, he
came to the king's palace. Sitting at the
entrance was a beggar in dirty rags,
calling out, "Help me, my son!" Filled
with pity, the young man gave the beggar
his good clothes and the money he had
saved for his return trip. Then, with
fearful heart, he entered the palace. When
he was escorted into the throne room, he
was shocked. Seated on the throne was
the beggar, wearing the clothes he had
just given him. The king smiled and said,
"Welcome, my son!"

What keeps me from responding the way
the young man did to the poor beggar?

*The princes among us are those
who forget themselves and serve [others].*

WOODROW WILSON

WEEK 16
Day 7 _____

*[Jesus said,] "There was once a man
who was giving a great feast
to which he invited many people. . . .
But they all began . . . to make excuses."*

LUKE 14:16, 18

In his meditation exercise called "Three
Classes of People," Saint Ignatius describes
three groups of people. Each desires to
follow Jesus faithfully, but each has an
attachment to something that is a barrier
to their desire. The first group might be
called the "dreamers." Since they love
their attachment too much, they do nothing
about it. The second group might be called
the "dodgers." They love their attachment
deeply, but they decide to go halfway.
They decide to pray every day that it
won't keep them from following Jesus.
The third group might be called the
"doers." They also love their attachment.
But unlike the first two groups, they
decide to do whatever is necessary to rid
themselves of it.

Which group of people do I tend
to fall into most of the time?

*Plunge into the deep without fear—and
with the gladness of April in your heart.*
RABINDRANATH TAGORE

WEEKLY MEETING
Sharing Agenda

1 Is there a "snail" that I have ingested into my system and need to expel, if I am to follow Jesus more faithfully and live out his plan for me? Can I identify the "snail"?

2 Can I recall giving up something I had always dreamed of, because it conflicted with a duty to love?

3 To what extent am I prone to get lost in my own little world and let my little problems blind me to the bigger ones of people around me?

4 How open am I to the option of saying yes to the things Lincoln did, if that is what God asks me to do?

5 In what way might I be more of a fan of Jesus than a follower?

6 What keeps me from responding the way the young man did to the poor beggar?

7 Which group of people in Saint Ignatius' exercise do I tend to fall into most of the time?

17 Why did Jesus submit to baptism and temptation?

Not far from the Dead Sea there is a shallow spot in the Jordan River. It was used as a crossing for caravans from all over the Near East. People used to gather there to exchange world news.

One day a new attraction sent people to the crossing. A man dressed like the prophets of old began to preach there. His name was John; and he told the people, "Turn away from your sins and be baptized" (LUKE 3:3).

Suddenly Jesus waded into the water to be baptized. John tried to stop him, saying, " 'I ought to be baptized by you. . . .' But Jesus answered him, 'Let it be so for now' " (MATTHEW 3:14-15).

And so John baptized Jesus. Then Jesus left the Jordan and went into the desert, "where he was tempted by the Devil" (LUKE 4:2).

This week's meditations focus on Jesus' baptism by John and his temptations by the devil. They invite you to ask, If Jesus was sinless, why did he ask to be baptized? If he was the Son of God, why did he allow

<u>the devil to tempt him?</u> The grace you ask
for is:

Lord Jesus, teach me
why you were baptized and tempted,
so that I may love you more dearly
and follow you more nearly.

Weekly Instruction

At this point it might be good to say a few
words about distractions. What should
you do when they occur during prayer?
Saint Francis de Sales answers:

"Bring your wayward heart
back home calmly and quietly.
Return it tenderly to its Master's side.
If you did nothing during prayer
but return your heart faithfully
and patiently to the Master's side,
your time of prayer would be well spent."

Daily Reading

1	This is the one	Mt 12:17–21
2	Right with God	Rom 5:1–4
3	Food you know not of	Jn 4:31–38
4	All else is garbage	Phil 3:7–11
5	What does it profit me	Mk 8:31–38
6	Jesus understands	Heb 4:14–16
7	Be patient	Jas 5:7–11

WEEK 17
Day 1 _____

[After Jesus was baptized,]
heaven was opened,
and the Holy Spirit came down upon him
in bodily form like a dove.
And a voice came from heaven,
"You are my own dear Son."

LUKE 3:21-22

Luke's account of Jesus' baptism contains
a beautiful reference to God as Trinity:
• Father ("a voice came from heaven"),
• Jesus ("You are my own dear Son"),
• Holy Spirit ("bodily form like a dove").
The mystery of the Trinity says that in
God are *three persons:* Father, Son, and
Holy Spirit. The Father is God, the Son
is God, and the Holy Spirit is God. Yet
there are not three Gods, *but only one.*

Which person of the Trinity do I relate to
best: Father, Son, or Holy Spirit? Why?
Which do I relate to least? Why?

Saint Patrick used the shamrock
(one leaf with three petals)
to illustrate the mystery of the Trinity.
A modern theologian
used the chemical compound H_2O.
It is one substance that exists
in three separate forms:
liquid (water), solid (ice), vapor (steam).

God looks down from heaven. . . .
Not one [person] does what is right,
not a single one.

PSALM 53:2-3

People ask, "Why was Jesus baptized?"
Obviously, it was not because he was a
sinful human being who needed
forgiveness. Rather, it was because he
was a member of a sinful human family
that needed forgiveness. Jesus asked to
be baptized because he had identified
himself so totally with the human family.
He could not stand apart from it—not even
from its sins. Jesus' action reminds us
that we, too, are members of the sinful
human family. We, too, cannot stand
apart from it, especially from its "family"
sins—disregard of the poor, neglect of the
environment, destruction of human life.

Do "family" sins tend to depress me
rather than challenge me?
How involved am I in them, personally?

Racism is yours, end it.
Injustice is yours, correct it. . . .
Ignorance is yours, banish it.
War is yours, stop it. . . .
The dream is yours, claim it.

WALTER FAUNTROY

WEEK 17
Day 3

*[After he was baptized, Jesus] was led
by the Spirit into the desert, where he
was tempted by the Devil for forty days.
In all that time he ate nothing,
so that he was hungry. . . . The Devil said
to him, "If you are God's Son,
order this stone to turn into bread."
But Jesus answered, "The scripture says,
'Man cannot live on bread alone.' "*

LUKE 4:1-4

Mary Jo Tully describes what life was like
during the Great Depression. She says,
"We lived from payday to payday. Mom
would often wait for Dad to come home
on payday before she could purchase the
food for the evening meal. Still, in what
he called his 'Irish wisdom,' Dad never
came home on payday without something
that would feed what he considered a
'deeper need.' One day it might be a bunch
of daisies. On another, a box of chocolates.
Once it was even an additional mouth to
feed—a puppy."

What "deeper need" do I have besides
"bread alone"? How do I try to satisfy it?

*When my spirit soars,
my body falls on its knees.*
GEORG CHRISTOPH LICHTENBERG

The Devil took [Jesus] up and
showed him in a second all the kingdoms
of the world. "I will give you
all this power and all this wealth . . .
if you worship me." Jesus answered,
"The scripture says, 'Worship the Lord
your God and serve only him.' "

LUKE 4:5–8

Joan Mills never knew her father. He died
when she was still very young. Her only
concrete link with him was a box of his
belongings in the attic. One day she felt
moved to explore it. She writes:
"I read a journal my father started at
seventeen. . . . He had left home . . .
and enrolled at Boston University.
By midwinter, he has worn out his one pair
of shoes and bought books instead of a
blanket. He drinks mugs of water to still
his hunger. A four-page entry celebrating
his discovery of the great poets ends,
'I have not eaten today.' "

How ready am I to deny my body
in favor of my spirit—
and to carry out God's plan for me?

The body, that is but dust;
the soul, it is a bud of eternity.
NATHANIEL CULVERWEL

WEEK 17
Day 5 —————————————————

*[Jesus said,] "The Son of Man did not come
to be served; he came to serve and
to give his life to redeem many people."*

MARK 10:45

Jesus' temptations preview how he will
carry out his mission. First, his refusal
to turn stones into bread previews that
he will not use his power for his own
personal comfort. Rather, he will sweat,
hunger, and suffer, just like us. Second,
his refusal to throw himself from the
Temple and let the angels catch him
previews that he hasn't come to be served
by others, but to serve them. Finally, his
refusal to kneel before the devil, even in
exchange for the whole world, previews
that he will not barter with evil. God is
God; right is right; wrong is wrong. Jesus
will die at the hands of evil rather than
barter with it.

How do I, sometimes,
tend to barter with evil—
or, at least, am tempted to do so?

*The face of Christ . . . shows us
the one thing we need to know—
the character of God.*

P. CARNEGIE SIMPSON

We have a High Priest
who was tempted in every way
that we are, but did not sin.

HEBREWS 4:15

In 1982 Archbishop Glemp of Warsaw
urged Polish young people not to give in
to the temptation to stop working for
political change in Poland. He told them
that he could sympathize with them,
because he had been beaten by police in
his youth for seeking similar change. Also,
his father had been punished for pressing
for political change. Just as Archbishop
Glemp could appreciate the temptations
of the Polish youth, so Jesus can appreciate
the temptations that each of us experiences.

What is one temptation I experience?
What might Jesus say about it?

We are no more responsible
for the evil thoughts
that pass through our minds
than a scarecrow is
for the birds that fly over
the seedplot it has to guard.
The sole responsibility in each case
is to prevent them from settling.

JOHN CHURTON COLLINS

WEEK 17
Day 7 _____

*When the Devil finished tempting Jesus
in every way, he left him for a while.
Then Jesus returned to Galilee, and the
power of the Holy Spirit was with him.*

LUKE 4:13-14

Native Americans went on *vision
quests.* They went off alone to pray and fast for
days to seek enlightenment from the
Spirit. One time a young brave returned
from such a quest without enlightenment.
An old brave said to him, "You stalked
your vision as you stalk deer. Stalking
alone does not bring vision; nor does
fasting or will power alone. Vision comes
as a gift born of humility, wisdom, and
patience. If your *vision quest* taught you
only this, it taught you much." As a result
of his desert experience, Jesus could say
to us what the old brave told the young
brave: "When you go off in quest of God's
will, remember that the 'vision' of that
will is 'a gift born of humility, wisdom,
and patience.' "

Am I, perhaps, stalking God's will as the
young brave stalked his "vision quest"?

*With time and patience
the mulberry leaf becomes a silk gown.*

CHINESE PROVERB

WEEKLY MEETING
Sharing Agenda

1 Which person of the Trinity do I relate to best: Father, Son, or Holy Spirit? Why? Which do I relate to least? Why?

2 Do "family" sins tend to depress me rather than challenge me? How involved am I in them?

3 What "deeper need" do I have besides "bread alone"? How do I satisfy it?

4 How ready am I to deny my body to strengthen my spirit—and to carry out God's plan for me?

5 How do I, sometimes, tend to barter with evil—or, at least, am tempted to negotiate with it?

6 What is a temptation I experience? What might Jesus say about it?

7 Am I, perhaps, stalking God's will as the young brave stalked his "vision quest"?

18   What did Jesus teach about how I should live?

Tom Dooley captured the imagination of the world in the 1950s. Fresh out of medical school and the navy, he went to Asia to serve among the very poor.

Tom's family was wealthy, and he enjoyed the good life. Commenting on this in *Guideposts* magazine, he says:
"There was plenty of money; I had my own horse, went to school abroad, studied to be a concert pianist."

But Tom's family was also deeply religious. He wrote:
"We were the prayingest family. . . .
We prayed when we got up . . .
when we sat down to eat,
when we finished eating,
when we went to bed."

Tom's family was also a Bible-reading family. Tom's favorite Bible reading was the Beatitudes in the Sermon on the Mount. He wrote:
"I loved the Beatitudes because they talked about what I was interested in.
Blest means 'happy,'
and that's just what I wanted to be.
Here were the rules for happiness."

This week's meditation exercises focus on the Beatitudes. The grace you ask for is:

*Father, help me take to heart
your Son's teachings
that I may know him more clearly,
love him more dearly,
and follow him more nearly.*

Weekly Instruction

The Bible readings for this week are all from the Sermon on the Mount (MATTHEW 5:1-7:29). Should you decide to read them, you might do so creatively.

For example, imagine yourself sitting on the mount with hundreds of people. Some are lame; some are blind; some are old. Study their faces as Jesus talks to their hearts. Study Jesus' face as he touches their hearts by his preaching.

Daily Reading

1	The Beatitudes	Mt 5:1-12
2	Salt and light	Mt 5:13-16
3	Moses and the prophets	Mt 5:17-20
4	Making up with others	Mt 5:21-24
5	Revenging others	Mt 5:38-42
6	Judging others	Mt 7:1-6
7	Living God's word	Mt 7:24-27

WEEK 18
Day 1 _____

[Jesus said,] "Happy are those who mourn;
God will comfort them!"

MATTHEW 5:4

Tom Dooley was moved to work among
Asia's poor while he was in the navy. One
day his ship picked up a boatload of sick
and wounded refugees drifting off the
coast of Vietnam. Tom discovered that the
simplest medical treatment brought smiles
to their pain-filled faces. He also discovered
that helping them made him happier than
he'd ever been in his life. After his hitch
in the navy, Tom went back to Asia. One
day he told a friend that his favorite
Beatitude was "Happy are those who
mourn." He explained that the word
mourn didn't mean "to be unhappy." It
meant "to be more aware of sorrow than
of pleasure." He added that if you try to
alleviate people's sorrow, "you can't help
but be happy. That's just the way it is."

How sensitive am I to the sorrow
in the lives of people around me?
When was the last time
I tried to alleviate someone's sorrow?

Who lives for himself is apt
to be corrupted by the company he keeps.

AUTHOR UNKNOWN

[Jesus said,]
"Blessed are the poor in spirit,
for theirs is the kingdom of heaven."

MATTHEW 5:3 (NRSV)

The movie *Quo Vadis,* starring Deborah
Kerr, dealt with the persecution of
Christians in ancient Rome. One day,
after a dangerous filming session, a reporter
asked Deborah, "Weren't you afraid when
the lions rushed you in the arena?"
Deborah replied, "Not at all! I'd read
the script, and I knew I'd be rescued."
This is the kind of childlike trust
that the "poor in spirit" had in God in
Jesus' time. To be "poor in spirit" meant
to be *detached* from material things and
attached to God alone. It meant to put
all one's trust in God rather than
in material things. To be "poor in
spirit" meant to have and to value only
one possession: God.

To what extent—and why—do I tend
to seek happiness and put my trust
in things rather than in God?

We are rich
in proportion to the number of things
we can do without.

HENRY DAVID THOREAU (slightly adapted)

WEEK 18
Day 3 _____

[Jesus said,]
"Happy are those who work for peace;
God will call them [God's] children!"
                                    MATTHEW 5:9

Jim McGinnis tells how two brothers were
screaming at each other as they played
on the sidewalk in front of his house. One
was on a tricycle; the other was blocking
the path of the tricycle. Jim asked the boys
if they were having fun. They said that
they were not. Then he asked them what
they might do to have fun. "We could take
turns riding the tricycle for about ten
minutes each," said the one child. When
Jim offered to time their rides, they both
smiled and got all excited. The younger
one even offered to let his older brother
ride first.

When two people are screaming,
do I use the occasion to prove
I can scream, too?
Or do I use the occasion to prove
there's a better way to settle disputes?

It takes two sides
to make a lasting peace,
but it takes only one
to take the first step.
                    EDWARD M. KENNEDY

[Jesus said,] "Happy are those
who are merciful to others;
God will be merciful to them!"
MATTHEW 5:7

An American and a Japanese embraced in
a Tokyo airport. The last time they met
was forty years ago in an Okinawan cave.
At that time, the American, Ponich, was
holding a child who had been shot in both
legs. The Japanese, Ishiboshi, leaped out
of the darkness and aimed his rifle at
Ponich. There wasn't a thing Ponich could
do, so he lay the child down, took out his
canteen, and began to wash the wounds.
An amazed Ishiboshi lowered his rifle.
When Ponich finished, he bowed to
Ishiboshi in gratitude and carried the
child to an American field hospital. In
1985 Ponich wrote a letter to a Tokyo
newspaper to thank the unknown soldier
who mercifully spared his life forty years
earlier. Ishiboshi saw the letter, and the
paper arranged their reunion.

What is an opportunity I have, right now,
for showing mercy to another?

We cannot, indeed, give like God,
but surely we may forgive like [God].
LAURENCE STERNE

WEEK 18
Day 5 _____

[Jesus said,] "Happy are you when people
insult you and persecute you . . .
because you are my followers."

MATTHEW 5:11

German submarine commander Martin
Niemoller was awarded the Iron Cross for
his service in World War I. After the war
he studied for the ministry and was
ordained. Before World War II, Niemoller
backed the Nazi party. But when he saw
the direction it began to take, he denounced
it publicly, was arrested, and was sent to
a concentration camp. Miraculously, he
survived eight years of imprisonment.
After the war, he lectured in behalf of
world peace. At one talk he was brutally
heckled and insulted for asking pardon of
the Jews. He reacted by imitating Jesus'
disciples, who rejoiced that God "considered
them worthy to suffer disgrace for the
sake of Jesus" (ACTS 5:41).

How do I react
when I am belittled or insulted?
What keeps me from reacting
as Jesus taught his disciples to do?

Ignore people who belittle you;
they're only trying to cut you down
to their size.   ANONYMOUS

*[Jesus said,] "Happy are those
whose greatest desire
is to do what God requires;
God will satisfy them fully!"*

MATTHEW 5:6

The great American concert violinist
Fritz Kreisler said:
"I was born with music in my system.
It was a gift from God. I didn't acquire it.
So I do not even deserve thanks
for the music.
Music is too sacred to be sold,
and the outrageous prices
charged by musical celebrities today
are truly a crime against society.
I never look upon the money I earn
as my own. It is public money.
It is only a fund entrusted to me
for proper disbursement.
My beloved wife feels exactly as I do. . . .
In all these years of my so-called
success in music we have not built
a house for ourselves. Between it and us
stand all the homeless in the world."

How fully do I agree with Kreisler?

*Serve one another with whatever gift
each of you has received.*

1 PETER 4:10 (NRSV)

WEEK 18
Day 7

[Jesus said,] "Happy are the pure in heart; they will see God!"

MATTHEW 5:8

One Halloween night, Tom Lewis was trying—with little success—to prepare a talk. He was constantly interrupted by a parade of trick-or-treat children. Toward the end of the night, Tom ran out of candy and cookies. He prayed that the doorbell would not ring again. But it did. And there stood his next-door neighbor with her three-year-old child. With total embarrassment, Tom poured out his predicament. And with total compassion and unselfishness, the three-year-old opened her bag of treats and said, "That's okay, Mr. Lewis. I'll give you some of my candy and cookies."

Am I more compassionate and unselfish than I used to be? How might I develop these basic ingredients of a pure heart?

People may excite in themselves
a glow of compassion, not by toasting
their feet at the fire and saying,
"Lord, teach me more compassion,"
but by going and seeking
an object that requires compassion.

HENRY WARD BEECHER

WEEKLY MEETING
Sharing Agenda

1 How sensitive am I to the sorrow in the lives of people around me? When was the last time I tried to alleviate someone's sorrow?

2 To what extent—and why—do I tend to seek happiness and put my trust in things rather than in God?

3 When two people are screaming, do I use the occasion to prove I can scream, too? Or do I use the occasion to prove there's a better way to settle disputes?

4 What is an opportunity I have, right now, to show mercy to another?

5 How do I react when I am belittled or insulted? What keeps me from reacting as Jesus taught us to?

6 How fully do I agree with Fritz Kreisler that "the money I earn . . . is only a fund entrusted to me for proper disbursement"?

7 Am I more compassionate and unselfish than I used to be? How might I develop these two basic ingredients of a pure heart?

19 How ready am I to love as Jesus loved?

In the movie *Shadow of the Hawk,* a young couple and an Indian guide are making their way up a mountainside. At one point the young woman slumps to the ground and says, "I can't take another step." The young man lifts her to her feet and says, "But, darling, we must go on. We have no other choice." She shakes her head and says, "I can't do it."

Then the Indian guide says to the young man, "Hold her close to your heart. Let your strength and love flow out of your body into hers." The young man does this, and in a few minutes the woman smiles and says, "Now I'm ready. I can go on."

We can all relate to that incident. There have been times in life when we, too, thought we couldn't go on. Then someone held us close to their heart and let their strength and love flow into us.

This week's meditations focus on love. The grace you ask for is:

Father, let your knowledge and love
of your Son flow into me,
that I may see him more clearly,
love him more dearly,
and follow him more nearly.

Daily Reading

As a change of pace, you might imagine
this week's daily readings to be letters
from God, written to you personally.

You might experiment with reading them
in a whisper or low voice. Some people
find that this gives them an impact that
silent reading can't give.

After you finish each daily reading, pause
momentarily to let it soak into your
heart—as water soaks into parched soil
after a refreshing shower.

1	Love your neighbor	Lk 10:25–37
2	Love as I love you	Jn 15:9–17
3	Love your enemies	Lk 6:27–36
4	Primacy of love	1 Cor 13
5	God is love	1 Jn 4:7–21
6	God's love for us	Rom 8:31–39
7	Proof of God's love	Jn 3:14–15

3 important factors in communication
① Praise
② expressing gratitude

WEEK 19
Day 1 *③ saying "I understand"*

Our love
should not be just words and talk;
it must be true love,
which shows itself in action.

1 JOHN 3:18

"Metamorphosis" is the story of an unmarried man named Gregor, who lives with his parents and sister. For years he's been a salesman, a slave to his customers and his boss. Although he is laughing on the outside, he is crying on the inside. He feels like an insect. Each night he dreams of his insectlike life. One morning he wakes up to discover that he's become what he feels like: a giant cockroach. The tragedy is that the only way Gregor can become human again is if he is loved by humans, especially his family. But his appearance makes this impossible. The greater part of the story deals with Gregor's pathetic efforts to express himself to his family. In the end, he simply gives up and dies.

Who, perhaps, is a "Gregor" in my life?

No greater burden can be borne
by an individual than to know
that no one cares or understands.

ARTHUR H. STANBACK

I think sometimes we do not listen to those we love.

Love is patient and kind. . . .
Love never gives up.
— 1 CORINTHIANS 13:4, 7

Alan Loy McGinnis tells this story about
the author Dr. Norman Lobsenz. Young
Norman's wife was in the midst of a
serious illness, and the ordeal was taking
its toll on Norman. One night he was on
the verge of collapse when, suddenly, he
recalled an incident from his childhood.
One night when his mother had taken ill,
Norman got up around midnight to get a
drink of water. As he passed his parents'
bedroom, he saw his father sitting in a
chair on his mother's side of the bed. She
was fast asleep. Norman rushed into the
room and cried, "Daddy, is Mom worse?"
"No, Norman," his father said softly. "I'm
just sitting here watching over her, in
case she wakes up and needs something."
That long-forgotten incident from his
childhood gave Norman all the strength
he needed to carry on.

What episode from my childhood
is a source of strength to me?

The pains of love be sweeter far
Than all other pleasures are.
— JOHN DRYDEN

WEEK 19
Day 3 _____

 Love is not . . . selfish or irritable;
love does not keep a record of wrongs.

1 CORINTHIANS 13:5

In an interview just before the 1986
Academy Awards, Barbara Walters asked
President and Mrs. Reagan how they had
managed to keep their love alive for
thirty-five years. As they thought about
the question, Barbara tried to help them,
asking, "Was it because both of you were
so willing to give and take on a 50–50
basis?" The first lady broke into a gentle
laugh and said, "Oh my, married life
never breaks that evenly. Sometimes it's
more like 90–10. So often one of us has to
give up so much more than the other."
That was a high point in the interview. It
made an important point: When it comes
to love, you can't keep score. The day two
people start to keep score in marriage is
the day their marriage starts to die.

Do I consciously or unconsciously tend
to keep score in my love relationships?

 Pure love and prayer are learned
in the hour
when prayer has become impossible
and your heart has turned to stone.

THOMAS MERTON

"In the same way
a Levite . . . walked on by."
LUKE 10:32

A woman was standing on a curb, waiting
for the light to change. On the opposite
curb was a teenage girl. The woman
noticed that the girl was crying. When the
light changed, each started across the
street. Just as they were about to meet,
the woman's motherly instincts came
rushing to the surface. Every part of her
wanted to comfort that girl. But the
woman passed her by. She didn't even
greet her. Hours later the image of the
crying girl still haunted the woman. Over
and over she said to herself: "Why didn't
I say to her, 'Honey, can I help?' Sure, she
might have rejected me. But, so what!
Only a minute would have been lost, but
that minute would have let her know that
someone cared. Instead, I passed her by.
I pretended she didn't exist."

Is there someone, right now, to whom
I should be reaching out in love?
What might be a first step in doing so?

'Tis better to have loved and lost
than never to have loved at all.
ALFRED LORD TENNYSON

WEEK 19
Day 5 _____

As they looked on, a change came over
Jesus: his face was shining like the sun,
and his clothes were dazzling white.

MATTHEW 17:2

British TV celebrity Malcolm Muggeridge
went to India to film Mother Teresa's
nuns working with dying patients. His
camera crew didn't anticipate the poor
lighting in the building and failed to bring
extra lights. So they thought it useless to
film the sisters at work. But someone
suggested they do it anyway. Maybe some
footage would be usable. To everyone's
surprise, the film was spectacular. It was
illumined by a mysterious light.
Muggeridge believes the light resulted
from a "glow" of love radiating from the
sisters' faces. He sensed this "glow"
himself when he first entered the building.
He says it was "like the haloes that artists
have seen and made visible round the
heads of saints." He adds, "I find it not
at all surprising that the luminosity
should register on photographic film."

Can I recall ever seeing someone "glow
with love"? What might cause the glow?

Where love is, there is God also.

LEO TOLSTOY

God will put [God's] angels in charge of you to protect you wherever you go.

PSALM 91:11

Actor Jimmy Stewart describes an incident that took place as his bomber squadron prepared to leave for Europe during World War II. As the last minute ticked away, Jimmy sensed that his father wanted to say something. But nothing came out. Finally, his dad hugged him and left. Only later did Jimmy discover that his father had slipped a letter into his pocket. It went something like this: "Soon after you read this letter, you will be on your way to the worst of dangers. Let us both count on the promise contained in the enclosed psalm. . . . I love you more than I can tell you. [signed] Dad." Jimmy then read the psalm. These words stood out: "God will put [God's] angels in charge of you to protect you wherever you go."

What keeps me from better expressing my love, especially to those closest to me? What person in particular would benefit from my doing this?

There is no security on earth;
there is only opportunity.
— GENERAL DOUGLAS MacARTHUR

WEEK 19
Day 7 _____

I have been put to death with Christ . . .
so that it is no longer I who live,
but it is Christ who lives in me.

GALATIANS 2:19-20

The musical *Man of La Mancha* is based
on Miguel de Cervantes's novel *Don
Quixote.* Toward the end of the musical,
Quixote is dying. At his side is Aldonza,
a worthless woman whom he idealized
and called Dulcinea. Quixote loved her
with a pure love, unlike anything she had
previously experienced. When Quixote
breathes his last, Aldonza sings "The
Impossible Dream." When she finishes,
someone shouts, "Aldonza." She replies,
"My name is now Dulcinea." Thanks to
Quixote's love, the ugly Aldonza had died,
and the beautiful Dulcinea was born. Love
had transformed a worthless wretch into
a wonderful woman.

How does the impact of Quixote's love on
Aldonza mirror the impact of Jesus' love
on me? What does all this say to me?

He drew a circle that shut me out—
Heretic, rebel, a thing to flout,
But love and I had the wit to win;
We drew a circle that took him in.

EDWIN MARKHAM

WEEKLY MEETING
Sharing Agenda

1 The tragic story "Metamorphosis" invites me to ask: Is there, perhaps, a "Gregor" in my life? What might I do about it?

2 What episode from my childhood continues to be a source of strength for me—even to this day?

3 To what extent might I consciously or unconsciously be keeping score in my love relationships?

4 Is there someone, right now, to whom I should be reaching out in love?

5 Can I recall a time when I saw someone, literally, glow with love? Have I ever felt myself glowing in this way?

6 What keeps me from better expressing my love, especially to those closest to me? What person in particular would benefit from my doing this?

7 What message might the story of Aldonza hold for me at this particular moment in my life?

20 How ready am I to pray as Jesus prayed?

In 1909 Father Francis Keller took a long trip to Gillette, Wyoming. He had sent a letter to the Catholic settlers there telling them that he would celebrate Sunday Mass with them. Many settlers hadn't seen a priest in years.

After Mass, a man said to Father Keller, "Your train doesn't leave until late tonight. After you've made your rounds, let's take a horseback ride into the hills. They're beautiful this time of the year."

Later the two men rode into the hills. After an hour they saw a woman waving in the distance. As they rode up and she saw Father Keller's collar, a remarkable expression came across her face. She said, "Father, my brother is dying."

Her brother was inside a tent. He was about thirty-five years old and extremely thin. Father Keller heard the man's confession and anointed him. In those days every priest in the West carried a tiny capsule of holy oil for just such an emergency. As soon as the priest finished, the young man closed his eyes in deep peace. He was dead.

Later the woman said to Father Keller, "Nobody told me that you were in Gillette today. But all his life my brother has prayed that a priest would be present at his death. This morning we prayed one last time for this grace."

That incredible story recalls the words of the poet Alfred Lord Tennyson: "More things are wrought through prayer than this world dreams of."

This week's meditations focus on prayer. The grace you ask for is:

Lord, teach me to pray that I come to know you more clearly,
love you more dearly,
and follow you more nearly.

Weekly Instruction

"The Three Hermits" is a Russian folktale about three monks living on an island. According to Leo Tolstoy, who tells the story, miracles sometimes occurred during the prayer of these simple monks. Their only prayer was:

"We are three;
you are three;
have mercy on us."

When the bishop heard about the three monks, he decided to visit them to teach them to pray in a more appropriate way. After he had finished instructing them, he set sail again for the mainland.

Suddenly, the bishop saw a ball of light chasing his boat. It was the three monks running across the water. When they got to the boat, they said, "We have forgotten part of your instruction and want to check it with you."

The bishop shook his head and said humbly, "Forget what I taught you and continue to pray in your old way."

That story makes an important point about prayer: <u>Keep your prayer simple. Whatever confuses or complicates prayer is probably best forgotten.</u> Father Daniel Lord was right when, at the end of his life, he gave this advice to a young person:

"Keep your prayer simple.
Talk to God as to a father,
to Christ as to a brother,
and to the Holy Spirit
as a constant companion."

Daily Reading

You might begin each reading this week with these words from the First Book of Samuel:

"Speak, LORD, your servant is listening."

1 SAMUEL 3:9

1	Prayer instruction	Lk 11:1–13
2	Persevering in prayer	Lk 18:1–8
3	Two pray-ers	Lk 18:9–14
4	Hilltop prayer	Lk 9:26–36
5	Lord's Prayer	Mt 6:7–13
6	Last Supper prayer	Jn 17:1–25
7	Gethsemane prayer	Mt 26:36–46

WEEK 20
Day 1 _____

[Jesus said,] "Ask, and you will receive."
LUKE 11:9

Bill was turning his young teacher, Mary,
into a nervous wreck. One morning before
school Mary sat writing something in
shorthand. Bill appeared and said,
"Whatdaya writing?"
Mary replied, "It's a prayer to God."
Bill joked, "Can God read shorthand?"
She replied, "God can do anything,
even answer this prayer."
With that, Mary stuck the note inside her
Bible and turned to write on the board.
As she did, Bill stole the note and put it
in his book. Years later Bill was sorting
through a box of old books and found the
note. He took it to the office for his
secretary to translate it. It read:
"Dear God, I can't handle my class
with Bill upsetting it. Touch his heart.
He's someone who can become either
very good or very evil."
Bill sat stunned, for only he knew how
accurate the prayer was and how well it
had been answered.

How do I feel about asking God for help?

 Pray to God, but row to the shore.
RUSSIAN PROVERB

[Jesus said,]
*"When you pray and ask for something,
believe that you have received it, and
you will be given whatever you ask for."*

MARK 11:24

Jim Johnson was sent to save a failing
hotel. The situation was so bad that Jim
decided upon desperate measures. Each
night he drove to a hill overlooking the
hotel. He parked, sat in the car, and
prayed for twenty minutes. He prayed for
the hotel guests, behind the lighted
windows. He prayed for the employees
and their families. He prayed for himself.
Gradually, changes started to take place
in the hotel. A new spirit radiated from its
employees. A new warmth greeted each
new guest. A new hope permeated the
operation. Within a year the hotel was
back on its feet. Norman Vincent Peale,
who tells the story, ends with this thought:
If the prayer of one person could revitalize
a hotel, think what the prayer of a nation
could do for the world.

What is my reaction to Peale's thought?

*Prayers travel more strongly
when said in unison.*

GAIUS PETRONIUS

WEEK 20
Day 3 _____

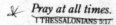

Pray at all times.
1 THESSALONIANS 5:17

French philosopher Blaise Pascal points out that God created us to be sharers in the divine power, not just spectators of it. Sharing in the divine power is one way we share in God's "image and likeness." Pascal points out further that a special way we share in the divine power is by prayer. He draws this parallel: Just as God shares power with us by making us *thinking* persons, so, too, God shares power with us by making us *praying* persons. Finally, few of us can impact human events significantly by our *thinking*, but all of us can do so by our *praying*.

Do I really believe that neglecting God's gift of prayer is as serious as neglecting God's gift of intelligence?

Prayer is the most powerful form of energy one can generate.
The influence of prayer
on the human mind and body
is as demonstrable
as that of secreting glands.
Prayer is a force
as real as terrestrial gravity.

Nobel prize winner ALEXIS CARREL

*[Jesus said to his disciples
in the garden of Gethsemane,]* ✳
*"The sorrow in my heart is so great
that it almost crushes me. . . ."
He went a little farther on,
threw himself face downward
on the ground, and prayed.*

MATTHEW 26:38-39

Just before the Battle of Gettysburg,
Lincoln became overwhelmed with fear.
He knelt and prayed. Later he said,
"Never had I prayed with such earnestness.
I wish I could repeat my prayer.
I felt that I must put all my trust
in Almighty God, who alone
could save the nation from destruction."
When Lincoln stood up, he said,
"I felt my prayer was answered. . . .
I had no misgiving about the result."

Have I ever felt so overwhelmed
with fear or concern
that I dropped to my knees to pray?

*Like a human parent,
God will help us when we ask for help,
but in a way that will make us
more mature, more real,
not in a way that will diminish us.*

MADELEINE L'ENGLE

WEEK 20
Day 5 _____

[Jesus] would go away to lonely places,
where he prayed.

LUKE 5:16

Adelaide Proctor's poem "A Legend" tells
about a monk whose preaching attracted
crowds and changed lives. Every time he
preached, an old man prayed for him. One
day the monk was thanking God for his
power to move hearts, when an angel
appeared and said to him:
"My son, it's not your preaching
that lights up hearts and changes people.
It's the old man's praying for you."
In other words, the monk's preaching
might be compared to the electrical cord
of a lamp. And the old man's prayer
might be compared to the current flowing
through it. Both are necessary if the lamp
is to light up.

Have I ever prayed that the Sunday sermon
would "light up hearts"?
Should I, perhaps, begin this practice?

Prayer is like
the turning of an electric switch.
It does not create the current;
it simply provides the channel
through which the electric current
may flow.   MAX HANDEL

[Jesus] looked up to heaven.
JOHN 17:1

In *The Inner Game of Tennis,* W. Timothy
Galwey points out that when we watch
tennis on TV, we see only the *outer* game:
the player's *body* in action. We don't see
the *inner* game: the player's *mind* in
action. Like tennis, prayer also has two
actions or dimensions: body (outer) and
mind (inner). The gospel refers to both
dimensions of Jesus' prayer: body and
mind. Referring to Jesus' body, it says he
knelt (LUKE 22:41), raised his eyes to heaven
(MARK 7:34), and prayed out loud (MATTHEW 26:42).
Referring to his mind, it says he used both
spontaneous thoughts from the heart
(JOHN 17:1) and *memorized* thoughts from the
psalms (MARK 15:34).

Do I ever experiment with my body
in prayer: kneeling, raising my eyes,
praying out loud? What are some helpful
things I have learned on how to improve
the quality of my prayer?

*Egyptian President Anwar Sadat
had a noticeable mark on his forehead.
He developed it by touching
his forehead to the ground so often
during the course of his daily prayer.*

*[Jesus said,] "This, then, is how
you should pray: 'Our Father . . . '"*

MATTHEW 6:9

Two things stand out in the Lord's Prayer:
• the word *Father* and
• the structure of the prayer.
The word for *father* that Jesus used was
Abba, a title of affection, much like our
word *daddy.* Jesus taught us to address
God with childlike affection and trust.
The structure of the Lord's Prayer divides
into two sets of requests:
• three "your" petitions—"Hallowed be
  your name," "your kingdom come,"
  "your will be done"—and
• three "our" petitions—"give us today
  our daily bread," "forgive us our
  trespasses," "deliver us from evil."
The "your" petitions look to the Father;
the "our" petitions, to ourselves. That is
the proper order for all true prayer.

How faithful am I to the practice of ending
my meditations with the Lord's Prayer?
How helpful do I find this?

*Hallowed be Thy name, not mine;
Thy kingdom come, not mine;
Thy will be done, not mine.*

DAG HAMMARSKJOLD

WEEKLY MEETING
Sharing Agenda

1 How do I feel about praying to God for help in time of need?

2 What is my reaction to Peale's story about Johnson's prayer and the thought that if the prayer of one person could revitalize a hotel, what might the prayer of a nation be able to do for the world?

3 To what extent do I agree that neglecting God's gift of prayer is as serious as neglecting God's gift of intelligence?

4 Have I ever felt so overwhelmed with fear or concern that I dropped to my knees to pray?

5 Have I ever prayed that the Sunday sermon would "light up hearts"? What are my thoughts about possibly beginning this practice?

6 Have I experimented with my body in prayer: kneeling, raising my eyes, praying out loud? What are some helpful things I have learned by trial and error through my daily meditation on how to improve the quality of my meditation?

7 How faithful am I to the practice of ending my meditations with the Lord's Prayer? How helpful do I find this?

21 How ready am I to serve as Jesus served?

Dr. Elisabeth Kubler-Ross is a former professor of psychiatry at the University of Chicago. She wrote a best-seller called *Death and Dying*. The book grew out of interviews with hundreds of people who had been declared clinically dead and then revived.

Repeatedly these people report that during their experience they underwent a kind of instant replay of their lives. It was like seeing a movie of everything they had ever done. How did the instant replay affect these people? Did it reveal anything significant?

Commenting on this, Dr. Kubler-Ross says:

"When you come to this point [the moment of leaving this life], you see there are only two things that are relevant: the service you rendered to others and love. All those things we think are important, like fame, money, prestige, and power, are insignificant."

This week's meditations focus on loving service. The grace you ask for is summed

up beautifully in this prayer attributed to
Saint Ignatius of Loyola:

Lord, teach me to be generous.
Teach me to serve you as you deserve;
to give and not to count the cost;
to fight and not to heed the wounds;
to toil and not to seek for rest;
to labor and not to ask for reward,
except to know
that I am doing your will.

Weekly Instruction

You might consider memorizing the above
prayer of Saint Ignatius and praying it
occasionally during the day—while waiting
for a red light to change or while jogging.
You might also consider making a
photocopy of it, cutting it out, and placing
it in your wallet.

Of course, these are merely suggestions.

Daily Reading

1	What does God want	Is 58:5-12
2	Who is the greatest	Mk 10:35-45
3	Wash another's feet	Jn 13:1-17
4	Reversal of fortunes	Lk 16:19-31
5	Who is my neighbor	Lk 10:25-37
6	See that justice is done	Is 1:10-17
7	I was hungry	Mt 25:31-46

WEEK 21
Day 1 _____

"I was hungry and you fed me."
MATTHEW 25:35

An old monk prayed many years for a vision from God. It came one day, just at the minute the monk was scheduled to feed the poor who gathered daily at the monastery gate. If he didn't show up with food, the people would leave, thinking the monastery had nothing to give them that day. The monk was torn between his duty to the poor and his heavenly vision. Then, with a heavy heart, he made his decision: He would feed the poor. An hour later, the monk returned to his room. When he opened the door, he could hardly believe his eyes. There was the vision, waiting for him. It smiled and said,
"My son, had you not gone to feed the poor, I would not have stayed."

How might this story apply to my life?

*Let those who are searching for God
visit the prison
before going to the temple.
Let them visit the hospital
before going to church.
Let them feed the hungry
before reading the Bible.*

TOYOHIKO KAGAWA (slightly adapted)

"[I was] thirsty and you gave me a drink."
MATTHEW 25:35

Eddie Fischer knew the kind of questions
television reporters would ask him:
"Why are you walking from Guatemala
to Pennsylvania?"
"I'm trying to raise money for a water
system in Rabinal, where thirty thousand
Indians have had no safe water supply
since the earthquake."
"Why did a college student, like you,
go to Rabinal in the first place?"
"I volunteered to help rebuild their water
system. A new one costs $300,000,
and they didn't have that kind of money.
So when my return plane ticket came due,
I got a refund and decided to try
to raise the money by walking home."
Eddie arrived home six months and four
thousand miles later. His "Water Walk"
raised exactly $300,000.

What keeps me from volunteering some
of my time to help unfortunate people?

Use what talents you possess:
the woods would be very silent
if no birds sang there
except those that sang best.
HENRY VAN DYKE

WEEK 21
Day 3 _____

"I was a stranger and you received me."

MATTHEW 25:35

Roy Popkin tells a true story about an old man who collapsed on a Brooklyn street corner and was rushed to Kings County Hospital. After some amateur detective work, a nurse located what seemed to be the man's son, who was a marine stationed in North Carolina. When the marine arrived, the nurse said to the old man, "Your son's here." The old man, now heavily sedated, reached out his hand feebly. The marine took it and held it tenderly for the next four hours. Occasionally the nurse suggested the marine take a break, but he refused. About dawn the old man died. After he passed away, the marine said to the nurse, "Who was that man?" The nurse said, "Wasn't he your father?" "No," said the marine, "but I saw he was dying and needed a son badly, so I stayed."

When was the last time
I went out of my way to be with another,
simply because that person needed me?

*If you haven't got charity in your heart,
you have the worst kind of heart trouble.*

BOB HOPE

"[I was] naked and you clothed me."
MATTHEW 25:36

Sister Emmanuelle lives among the ten thousand garbage pickers in Cairo. These people survive by scouring the city's garbage dump. Sister's day begins at four-thirty as she wakes in a hut with a hole in the roof. After washing in a bucket of water, she walks two miles to attend Mass. That walk takes her past piles of rotting garbage and snarling dogs. At nine o'clock she begins teaching Arabic to about forty children. She ends by teaching them how to pray. Then she visits families, writing down their pressing needs in a notebook. Sister Emmanuelle is a gentle person, says *Time* magazine. But "her gentleness turns to steel when she browbeats the bureaucrats and the bankers to help her garbage pickers."

Have I ever considered giving my life—or a part of it—in service to the poor, as Sister Emmanuelle is doing?

Great souls aren't those
with less passion and greater virtue
than other souls,
but only those with greater designs.
FRANCOIS DE LA ROCHEFOUCAULD

WEEK 21
Day 5 _____

"I was sick and you took care of me."
MATTHEW 25:36

An old native in New Guinea used to read gospel stories to outpatients while they waited to be treated at the missionary clinic. One day he experienced trouble reading. The doctor checked his eyes and found that the man was rapidly going blind. The next day the old man didn't show up at the hospital. Someone said he had gone off to the hills alone. A week later a boy led the doctor to the old man's hideout. "What are you doing here?" asked the doctor. The old man replied, "While I still have eyesight, I wanted to spend all my time memorizing stories and passages from the Bible. When I lose my sight completely, Doctor, I'll be back at the hospital again, telling outpatients about Jesus."

What makes me reluctant to share the good news of Jesus with others as enthusiastically as the old man did?

[Jesus said,]
"If [my disciples] keep quiet,
the stones themselves
will start shouting."
LUKE 19:40

"[I was] in prison and you visited me."
MATTHEW 25:36

Saint Peter Claver was a Jesuit priest.
He worked among the black slaves
in seventeenth-century South America.
Peter wrote in a letter to a friend:
"Yesterday . . .
a great number of black people,
seized along the African rivers,
were put ashore from a large ship.
We hurried out with two baskets full
of oranges, lemons, sweet biscuits. . . .
A number of blacks were lying on mud . . .
naked without any covering at all.
We took off our cloaks, went to a store,
brought from there all the wood available
and put it together to make a platform.
Then forcing our way through the guards,
we eventually managed to carry
all the sick to it." (slightly adapted)

When I try to imagine that I am a slave
lying naked and sick in the mud,
what are my thoughts as I lie there?

*A person can be as truly a saint
in a factory as in a monastery;
and there's as much need for a saint
in the one as in the other.*
ROBERT J. McCRACKEN (slightly adapted)

WEEK 21
Day 7

*"Whenever you did this
for one of the least important
of these brothers [or sisters] of mine,
you did it for me!"*

MATTHEW 25:40

By the time she was eighty years old,
Lorraine Hale had spent sixteen years
helping nearly six hundred babies
withdraw from drugs. These tiny victims
are born to junkie mothers and become
addicted in the womb. They shake, vomit,
suffer from bad diarrhea. It usually takes
four to six weeks for them to withdraw.
"Mother" Hale began this work in her
own house in Harlem, using her own
money. Sometimes she was caring for
twenty babies at one time. Her work went
largely unnoticed until President Reagan
heard about it. Soon she had a team of
helpers and a fully equipped center.

If I were in a situation like the one
Mother Hale found herself in—
broke, unable to buy food
for the babies in my care—
what would I say to God about it?

*Charity is a naked child,
giving honey to a bee without wings.*

FRANCIS QUARLES

WEEKLY MEETING
Sharing Agenda

1 How might the story about the monk who had a vision apply to me?

2 What keeps me from volunteering some portion of my time to help unfortunate people?

3 When was the last time that, like the marine, I went out of my way to be with another, simply because the person needed me?

4 Have I ever considered giving my life—or a part of it—in service to the poor, as Sister Emmanuelle has chosen to do?

5 What makes me reluctant to share the good news of Jesus with others as enthusiastically as the old blind man did?

6 What thoughts come to my mind as I imagine myself to be a naked, sick slave lying in mud, after having been taken from a slave ship?

7 What thoughts come to my mind as I imagine myself to be Mother Hale, without money to buy food or medicine for the babies in my care?

*Serving God and
other people.*

22 How closely do I want to journey with Jesus?
(Three Degrees of Humility)

An angel was walking down the street, carrying a torch in one hand and a pail of water in the other.

A woman asked the angel, "What are you going to do with the torch and with the pail?" The angel said, "With the torch, I'm going to burn down the mansions of heaven; and with the pail, I'm going to put out the fires of hell. Then we shall see who *really* loves God."

The angel's point is that many people follow Jesus more out fear (of hell) and hope (of heaven) than out of love (of God).

This week's meditations focus on your love of God. They try to help you discern how strong it is. The grace you ask for is:

Father,
bless me with a love
that will motivate me
to want to journey with Jesus
as closely as possible,
even to the point of experiencing poverty
and dishonor—as he did—
if this be for your greater glory.

Weekly Instruction

In his meditation called "Three Degrees
of Humility," on which this week's
meditations are based, Saint Ignatius
distinguishes three levels of loving God.

The first is the *essential* level. At this
level, we love God this much, at least:
There is no person or thing so attractive
that for that person or thing we would
offend God seriously. This level of love
invites us to pray with Saint Ignatius:

Lord, teach me to be generous.
Teach me to serve you as you deserve;
to give and not to count the cost;
to fight and not to heed the wounds;
to toil and not to seek for rest;
to labor and not to ask for reward,
except to know
that I am doing your will.

The second level of love is the *logical* level.
At this level, we love God so much that
we desire to please God in all that we do.
In other words, logic dictates that we do
more than not offend God. This level of
love invites us to pray with Ignatius:

Take, Lord,
and receive all my liberty, my memory,
my understanding, and my entire will—
all that I hold dear.

You have given all these things to me.
I now place them all at your service,
to be used as you wish.
Give me only your love and your grace.
These are enough for me.

The third level of love is the *folly* level.
At this level, we love God so much that
we are not content simply to please God.
We desire to do things for God that the
nonlover would consider foolish. For
example, we desire to follow God's Son
so perfectly that we prefer poverty to
wealth, because this makes us more like
Jesus, who lived a life of poverty. And we
prefer insults and rejection, because this
makes us more like Jesus, who was
insulted and rejected, even to the point of
being crucified between two criminals.
This level of love invites us to pray with
Saint Ignatius:

Lord, I ask to serve you:
first, with complete poverty of spirit,
even actual poverty if it pleases you;
and, second, I ask to serve you
in suffering insults and rejection,
to better imitate Jesus—
providing I can do this
without sin on anyone's part and if it be
for your greater honor and glory.

Obviously, this week's meditations are extremely important. You might feel moved to seek God's help to do them well by doing something special during this week. For example, you might attend Mass daily.

Again, this is only a suggestion. The important thing is to strive—in an extra special way—to open your heart to God's grace in the week ahead.

Daily Reading

1 Accept my apologies   Lk 14:16-24
2 Whom to fear   Mt 10:26-33
3 He will honor you   Jn 12:20-26
4 I bring a sword   Mt 10:34-39
5 He gave up everything   Phil 2:6-11
6 No greater love   Jn 15:12-17
7 Love born of forgiveness   Lk 7:36-50

230

*[Jesus said,] "Anyone who starts to plow
and then keeps looking back
is of no use for the Kingdom of God."*

LUKE 9:62

Christians come in three models: rafts,
sailboats, and tugboats. First, there are
the *rafts*. Basically, they are Christian in
name only. They follow Jesus only when
someone else pulls or pushes them. Second,
there are the *sailboats*. They follow Jesus,
but only in sunny weather. When stormy
weather comes, they go in the direction
of the wind and the waves. In other words,
they follow the crowd more than they
really follow Jesus. Finally, there are the
tugboats. They follow Jesus regardless of
the weather. They go in his direction not
only when the wind and the waves serve
them but also when the wind and waves
oppose them. Tugboats don't always travel
as fast as they should, but they always
travel straight.

What "model" am I?
If I were arrested for being a Christian,
would they find enough evidence
to convict me?

To be Christian is to be like Christ.

WILLIAM PENN (slightly adapted)

[Jesus said,]
"Who acknowledges me before others,
I will acknowledge before my Father."
MATTHEW 10:32 (NRSV)

Arthur Jones was drafted into the British Royal Air Force. The first night in boot camp he had to make a decision. Should he continue to kneel for his night prayers, as he always had done at home? He squirmed a little bit. Then he thought to himself, "Why should I change? Just because I'm away from home, am I going to start letting other people dictate my actions?" As it turned out, Arthur was the only Catholic in the barracks. Yet night after night he knelt. He said later that those ten minutes on his knees often sparked discussions that lasted for hours. His last night in boot camp, someone said, "You're the finest Christian I've ever met." Arthur disagreed but thanked the person anyway.

How much am I motivated by a concern for what my friends will think?
By a concern for what God will think?

What we need isn't more Christianity but more Christians who practice it.
E. C. McKENZIE

WEEK 22
Day 3 _____

[Jesus said,]
"My Father will honor anyone
who serves me."

JOHN 12:26

The film *Chariots of Fire* is based on the true story of Eric Liddell of England. He was favored to win the gold in the 100-meter event in the 1924 Olympics. Then came the bombshell. The event was scheduled to be run on Sunday, which violated Eric's religious convictions. When word got around England that Eric wouldn't run on Sunday, incredible pressure was put upon him to violate his conscience. But he held firm. Eventually Eric switched to the 400-meter event, a race he had never run in his life. Just before the event, Jackson Scholz, an American runner, handed Eric a note. It read: "My Father will honor anyone who serves me" (JOHN 12:26). Seconds later Eric won the the event. Still clutched in his hand was the note from Jackson Scholz.

Can I recall a time when I risked a great deal to be faithful to my beliefs?

The only tyrant I accept in this world
is the still voice within.

MOHANDAS K. GANDHI

Jesus . . . rebuked Peter.
"Get away from me, Satan," he said.
"Your thoughts don't come from God."

MARK 8:33

The play *A Man for All Seasons* is based
on the true story of Sir Thomas More. In
one scene Lord Norfolk tries to persuade
Thomas to sign a paper declaring that he
thinks the recent marriage of King Henry
VIII is valid. If More refuses, the king will
execute him for treason. When More
refuses, Norfolk cries out in frustation:
"Damn it . . . look at those names. . . .
You know these men! Can't you do what
I did and come with us for fellowship?"
Sir Thomas refuses again, putting his
loyalty to God ahead of everything, even
his own life.

Where am I currently feeling a pressure
from friends to follow their lead rather
than what I believe is right?

If a man
does not keep pace with his companions,
perhaps it is because he hears
a different drummer.
Let him keep step to music which he hears,
however measured or far away.

HENRY DAVID THOREAU

WEEK 22
Day 5 _____

*[The Son of God] gave up all he had,
and took the nature of a servant.*

PHILIPPIANS 2:7

A king fell in love with a peasant girl. But
it occurred to him that if he married her
and remained a king, the gap between
them might be too great. She might
always be conscious of the fact that he
was royalty and she was a lowly peasant.
So the king decided to resign his kingship
and become a lowly peasant himself. He
realized, however, that this plan could
backfire. People might think him a fool,
and the girl might reject him. He could
end up losing both his love and his throne.
But the king loved the girl so much that
he decided to risk everything to make the
marriage possible.

How is this story a parable of Jesus
and his love for me?
How much am I willing to risk in imitation
of Jesus, who risked so much for me?

*To reach the port of heaven,
we must sail sometimes with the wind
and sometimes against it—
but we must sail,
and not drift; nor lie in anchor.*

OLIVER WENDELL HOLMES

[Jesus said,]
"No one has greater love than this,
to lay down one's life for one's friends."
JOHN 15:13 (NRSV)

Colonel John Mansure tells this story in *Missileer* magazine. Mortar shells hit a Vietnam orphanage, wounding several of the children. An American navy doctor saw that one of the girls needed an immediate blood transfusion. Several unharmed children had the right blood type. Using pidgin Vietnamese, the doctor explained the need for blood and asked if anyone would give it. At first no one responded. Then a small boy slowly raised his hand. Quickly, the doctor swabbed his arm with alcohol, inserted the needle, and withdrew the blood. After it was all over, the boy began to cry. No amount of hugging would comfort him. Later it was discovered why. The boy had misunderstood that by giving his own blood, he himself would die.

How ready am I to imitate Jesus—even to giving my life for another?

✳ *It is possible to give without loving, but it is impossible to love without giving.*
RICHARD BRAUNSTEIN

WEEK 22
Day 7 _____

*[When Thomas saw the wounds
in the body of the risen Jesus,
he repented his doubts and cried out,]*
"My Lord and my God!"

JOHN 20:28

Piri Thomas was sharing a prison cell
with "the thin kid." One night Piri was
moved to repent his sinful life. He waited
until the kid was asleep. Then he knelt
down and prayed out loud. He writes:
"I told God what was in my heart. . . .
I talked to him plain. . . .
I talked to him of my wants and lacks,
of my hopes and disappointments."
After Piri finished praying, a voice said,
"Amen." It was "the thin kid." No one
spoke for a long time. Then the kid
whispered, "I believe in Dios also." The
two young men talked a long time. Then
Piri climbed back into his bunk, saying,
"Good night, Chico. I'm thinking that God
is always with us. It's just that we aren't
always with [God]."

How ready am I to repent my past
as Thomas did, and follow Jesus
as closely as possible in the future?

Choice, not chance, determines destiny.

E. C. McKENZIE

WEEKLY MEETING
Sharing Agenda

1　If I were arrested for being a Christian, what aspect of my behavior would be the best evidence that I was one?

2　How much am I motivated by a concern for what my friends will think? By a concern for what God will think?

3　Can I recall a time when I risked a great deal to be faithful to my beliefs?

4　Where am I currently feeling a pressure from friends to follow their lead rather than what I believe is right?

5　How is the story about the king and the peasant girl a parable of Jesus and his love for me? How much am I willing to risk in imitation of Jesus, who risked so much for me?

6　How ready am I to imitate Jesus—even to giving my life for another?

7　How ready am I to repent my past and follow Jesus as closely as possible in the future?

Discerning Gods
will in our lives

23 How ready am I to decide to journey with Jesus?

A fifteen-year-old boy and his father were driving past a tiny airport in Ohio. A low-flying plane suddenly spun out of control and nose-dived into the runway. The boy yelled, "Dad! Dad! Stop the car!"

Moments later the boy was pulling the pilot out of the plane. He was a twenty-year-old student flier who was practicing takeoffs and landings. The young man died in the boy's arms.

When the boy arrived home, he threw his arms around his mother and cried, "Mom, he was my friend! He was only twenty!"

That night the boy was too shocked to eat supper. He went to his room, closed the door, and lay on his bed. He had been working part-time in a drugstore. Every cent he made he spent on flying lessons. His goal was to get his pilot's license when he turned sixteen.

The boy's parents wondered what effect the tragedy would have on their son. Would he stop taking lessons, or would he continue? They agreed that the decision must be his.

Two days later the boy's mother brought some freshly baked cookies to her son's room. On his dresser she saw an open notebook. It was the one he had kept from childhood. Across the top of the page was written, in big letters, "The Character of Jesus." Beneath was listed a series of qualities:

"Jesus was sinless;
he was humble;
he championed the poor;
he was unselfish;
he was close to God . . ."

The mother saw that in her son's hour of decision he was turning to Jesus for guidance. Later she turned to her son and said, "What have you decided about flying?" The boy replied, "Mom, I hope you and Dad will understand, but with God's help, I must continue to fly."

That boy was Neil Armstrong. And on July 20, 1969, he became the first human being to walk on the moon. Few people who watched that historic event on television knew that one of the reasons Neil Armstrong was walking on the moon was Jesus. They didn't know that it was from Jesus that he drew strength and guidance to continue his flying.

Consider a second story. In January 1973, Joe Paterno, head coach at Penn State, was offered $1 million to coach the New England Patriots. He was thrilled by the offer and phoned Patriot owner Billy Sullivan to say he would meet with him in New York the following morning. That night Joe Paterno could not sleep.

The next morning, after deep reflection, Paterno phoned Sullivan and turned down the $1-million offer. Later he explained his decision to sports writers. He said the opportunity to impact the lives of college students was more important than the money and the prestige that he would get from being a pro coach.

Both of these stories involve important decisions. Both involve trying to discern God's will concerning what is the correct decision to make.

This week's meditations focus on discerning God's will concerning a decision you may wish to make. The grace you ask for is:

Lord, bless me with
the clarity of vision
to discern your will for me and
the courage of heart
to carry it out.

Weekly Instruction

How do you go about discerning God's will? For example, how do you learn God's will concerning your life's calling, as Armstrong did? Or how do you discern whether or not to make a change in your life's work, as Paterno did?

Saint Ignatius says there are three times when major decisions, like these, can be made.

The first time is when there is absolute *clarity* about what God's will is. Think of Saint Paul on the road to Damascus (ACTS 9:1-15). There was no doubt in his mind about what God wanted him to do.

The second time is when you experience *agitation* about what to do. Think of Joe Paterno being pulled one way, then the other. In times like this, you can "test" the pulls to see which is from God. For example, Paterno rightly concluded that the one that brought him inner peace was the right one.

The third time is when you experience *neither clarity nor agitation*. Think of Neil Armstrong. After the plane crash he experienced neither clarity nor agitation. He simply wanted to reassure himself about whether he should continue to fly or not. After weighing the pros and cons and praying, he decided to continue flying.

When it comes to this third decision time, Ignatius offers two procedures for discerning God's will. The first involves six steps.

1 Clarify the decision you must make and the choices that lie open to you.

2 Recall that your decision should be in accord with God's purpose in creating you: to share your life and love with God and with other people forever.

3 Pray for the grace to be open to the right choice.

4 List the pros and cons for each choice.

5 Determine which choice seems *more* in accord with God's purpose in creating you.

6 Make your decision, asking God to confirm (by the gift of inner peace) that it is the right one.

The second procedure involves five steps.

1 Ask yourself, Do the inner movements that I feel—for or against a choice— stem from my love for God or from some other source, for example, selfishness?

2 Imagine you are a person you have never met before. You take a liking to

this person and want the best for him
or her. Ask yourself, What would I
counsel this person to do if he or she
had to make the same decision I do?

3 Imagine yourself at the moment of
death. Ask yourself, Which choice will
likely give me greater joy at that time?

4 Imagine yourself before the judgment
seat of God after your death. Ask
yourself, Which choice will likely give
me greater joy then?

5 Make your decision, asking God to
confirm that it is the right one.

One final observation. Often you are not
faced with a decision about your life's
calling or a change in it. Rather, it's a
decision about how well you are living out
a choice already made. If you are not doing
it well, what change ought you to make?

Daily Reading

1 Ignoring the poor   Lk 16:19-31
2 They will hate you   Mt 10:16-25
3 Causing others to sin   Mt 18:6-9
4 He suffered for us   Is 53:3-8
5 The Good Shepherd   Jn 10:11-18
6 Reap the harvest   Lk 10:1-9
7 Salt and light   Mt 5:13-16

WEEK 23
Day 1

"Remember, my son, that in your lifetime you were given all the good things, while Lazarus got all the bad things."

LUKE 16:25

When he was thirty years old, Albert Schweitzer gave up a successful music career to become a missionary doctor in Africa. One gospel story that influenced his decision was the parable of Lazarus. It concerns a rich man who feasted daily while Lazarus lay at the gates of the man's house, begging for food. But the rich man ignored him, feasting his dogs instead. Then, Lazarus and the rich man both died. In the next world their plights were reversed. Only then did the rich man realize how terribly callous he had been. When Schweitzer read the parable, he reasoned that his African brother was Lazarus and he was the rich man. Then he asked himself, "How can I wallow in pleasure while my African brother writhes in pain?"

Have I ever felt as Schweitzer did?

Every action of our lives touches on some chord that will vibrate in eternity.

EDWIN HUBBEL CHAPIN

[Jesus said,]
*"For my sake you will be brought to trial
before rulers and kings."*

MATTHEW 10:18

A young South Korean poet, Kim Chi Ha,
was sentenced to life in prison for writing
poems critical of his nation's treatment
of the poor. Writing in *Maryknoll* magazine,
Kim Chi Ha's mother said she agrees
wholeheartedly with her son's statement
that "we must be for the poor
and oppressed of society.
Society puts these people down,
but the gospel tells us
they are important.
There is a real struggle against evil
in the world, and
we must take this struggle seriously."
Kim Chi Ha's mother concludes:
"I want to follow my son's statement. . . .
I want to identify with the oppressed,
the troubled, the despised. . . .
This is my dream, my faith."

How seriously do I take the struggle
against evil in the world?

*Apathy is the glove
into which evil slips its hand.*

BODIE THOENE

WEEK 23
Day 3 _____

[Jesus said,]
"Things that make people fall into sin
are bound to happen,
but how terrible for the one
who makes them happen!"

LUKE 17:1

Bubba Smith, former football star, is also famous for his beer commercials. In October 1985, Michigan State made him the grand marshal of its homecoming parade. Bubba was thrilled. As he rode through the student-lined streets, one side started shouting, "Tastes great." The other side shouted back, "Less filling." It was obvious that Bubba's beer commercials were a hit. That night Bubba was so disturbed by excessive drinking among students that he decided to stop making the commercials. He feared that he was influencing them to do something he didn't want to be a part of. That decision cost Bubba a lot of money, but he thought something much greater was at stake.

How ready am I to get involved
in the struggle against evil
in the world?

We are our choices.
JEAN-PAUL SARTRE

*It is by his [Christ's] wounds
that you have been healed,*
1 PETER 2:24

The novel *Great Expectations* concerns a
boy named Pip, who comes from a poor
family. One day Pip is kind to a stranger,
whom everyone else rejects. Months later
a lawyer shows up at Pip's home, saying
that Pip is to receive a large sum of money,
annually, from an anonymous donor.
There is one stipulation. Pip is to be sent
to London and educated in the best
schools. Pip's life changes beyond all his
dreams. Years later a crude, lower-class
man shows up at Pip's beautiful London
home. Pip is rude to him and tries to run
him off. Then comes the surprise. The
man turns out to be the stranger Pip
befriended years before. The man is also
the anonymous benefactor. He has
dedicated his life to hard work to give Pip
a new life. Pip is too repentant to speak.

How is this story a kind of parable
of what Jesus has done for me—
and what am I doing in return for Jesus?

*Who stays not in his littleness
loses his greatness.*
SAINT FRANCIS DE SALES

248

WEEK 23
Day 5

*Teach me, L*ORD, *. . . to serve you*
with complete devotion.

PSALM 86:11

Vietnam vet Charlie DeLeo got a job as a
maintenance worker at the Statue of
Liberty. He kept the two hundred glass
windows in the crown and torch clean and
made sure their sodium vapor lights were
working. Pointing to the torch, Charlie
said, "That's my chapel. . . . I go up there
on my breaks and meditate." One day he
wrote this prayer: "O Lord, I don't ever
expect to have the faith of Abraham . . .
nor the strength of Samson, nor the
courage of David . . . nor the wisdom of
Solomon. . . . But what I do expect,
O Lord, is your calling on me some day.
What is your will, I shall do; what is
your command shall be my joy. . . .
And I shall not fail you, O Lord,
for you are all I seek to serve."
(slightly adapted)

What impact does praying Charlie's prayer
slowly, in a low whisper, have on me?
Did I make it my prayer as well?

Who prays as he ought,
will endeavor to live as he prays.

JOHN OWEN

*[Jesus said,] "There is a large harvest,
but few workers to gather it in."*
LUKE 10:2

Francis Xavier was a high jumper at the
University of Paris. One day he was
deeply moved by Jesus' words, "Will a
person gain anything if he wins the whole
world but is himself lost or defeated?"
(LUKE 9:25). The more Francis thought
about that question, the more it haunted
him. Finally, he turned his back on
university life, entered a seminary, and
became a missionary to India. Writing to
a friend, he said: "Many out here fail to
become Christians only because there is
nobody prepared to undertake the task of
teaching them about Christ. I have often
felt moved to go to the universities of
Europe [to urge students to make] the
Spiritual Exercises of [Ignatius] to find
God's will in their hearts and to embrace
it . . . saying: 'Lord, here I am. What would
you have me to do?' "

How close am I to saying,
"Lord, here I am.
What would you have me to do?"

If it's going to be, it's up to me.
ROBERT H. SCHULLER

WEEK 23
Day 7 _____

*"I am now giving you
the choice between life and death. . . .
Choose life."*

DEUTERONOMY 30:19

Julius Caesar, William Shakespeare's masterful play, contains this passage:
"There is a tide in the affairs of men
Which, taken at the flood,
leads on to fortune;
Omitted, all the voyage of life
Is bound in shallows and in miseries."
Shakespeare's point is that there comes a time in life when we must take our destiny into our own hands and decide our future. You are face-to-face with such a decision right now. This meditation ends the second phase of *The Spiritual Exercises of Saint Ignatius.* One decision you must make is whether you want to go on to the third phase now or to take time off for a while and then decide.

This meditation invites you to look to your future. Is there any decision about your future that the Holy Spirit seems to be moving you to make? What is it?

 *God's kingdom is within;
only by searching within, will I find it.*

AUTHOR UNKNOWN

WEEKLY MEETING
_____ Sharing Agenda

1 Have I ever considered making a
   180-degree change in my life, as
   Schweitzer did?

2 How seriously do I take the struggle
   against evil in the world?

3 How ready am I to get involved in the
   struggle against evil in the world?

4 How is the story of what the stranger
   did for Pip a kind of parable of what
   Jesus has done for me? How might I be
   responding to Jesus as Pip did to his
   benefactor?

5 What impact did praying Charlie's
   prayer in a slightly audible voice have
   on me? To what extent was I able to
   make it my prayer?

6 How close am I to saying, "Lord, here
   I am. What would you have me to do?"

7 Is there any decision the Holy Spirit
   seems to be moving me to make? Also,
   what is my decision about going on to
   phase three of _The Spiritual Exercises
   of Saint Ignatius?_

III
JOURNEY

The "Third Week" of
The Spiritual Exercises of Saint Ignatius
focuses on this great mystery:
The second person of the Trinity,
in the person of Jesus,
suffered and was crucified for us.

This incredible mystery inspires us
to pray with Saint Ignatius:

Father, bless me
with the grace to experience
sorrow with the sorrow-filled Jesus,
anguish with the anguished-filled Jesus,
and grief with the grief-filled Jesus,
because of what he endures
for my sins.

24 How ready am I to be rejected as Jesus was?

Two music critics covered a concert by a
Russian pianist in New York City. The
critic for the *New York Times* summed
up the concert, saying,
"It was a disappointing evening.
One had hoped for more. . . .
Because of constant experimentation
with the tempos,
the work sounded disconnected."

The critic for the *New York Herald
Tribune* summed up the same concert in
these words:
"Two-thousand-candlepower playing
by the Soviet Thor of the piano . . .
electrified to cheers an audience
which uses its hands more often
to stifle yawns than to applaud."

These opposing reviews of the same
performance recall a line from Oscar
Wilde's *Reading Gaol:*
"Two men looked through prison bars—
one saw mud, the other stars."

Just as the two music critics and the two
prisoners had conflicting views, so did the
people have different views of Jesus.
Some heard and saw the things he did and

said, "He really is the Savior of the world" (JOHN 4:42). Other people heard and saw the same things and rejected Jesus, saying, "He's gone mad!" (Mark 3:21-22).

This week's meditations focus on people's rejection of Jesus—and the rejection you can also expect if you follow Jesus (JOHN 15:18, 20). The grace you ask for is:

*Father, bless me with the grace
to enter into the heart of Jesus and
to experience
the sorrow and grief that he did
when the people he loved dearly
rejected him.*

Weekly Instruction

This week's meditations set the stage for the events of Holy Week, the ultimate rejection of Jesus by the people he loved so profoundly.

Daily Reading

1 Rejection by friends   Lk 4:16–30
2 Rejection by others   Lk 7:29–35
3 More rejection   Mk 3:20–30
4 They refused to believe   Mk 6:1–6
5 They turned away   Jn 6:54–67
6 They plotted against him   Jn 11:45–57
7 They'll reject you also   Jn 15:18–25

WEEK 24
Day 1 ⎯⎯⎯⎯⎯⎯⎯⎯⎯⎯⎯

There was a division
in the crowd because of Jesus.
Some wanted to seize him.
JOHN 7:43-44

The Battle of Gettysburg left fifty thousand
dead or wounded. Months later, on
November 19, 1863, President Lincoln
delivered a brief dedication address at the
military cemetery at Gettysburg. The
Harrisburg *Patriot and Union* said of it,
"We pass over the silly remarks of the
President of the United States." The
Chicago *Times* said, "The cheek of every
American must tingle with shame as he
reads the silly, flat, and dish-watery
utterances of . . . the President of the
United States." Today, the Gettysburg
Address is considered one of the greatest
speeches of American history. In a similar
way, the words of Jesus were ridiculed by
some people of his time. But today, even
nonbelievers admit that "nobody has ever
talked" as Jesus did (JOHN 7:46).

How much does fear of rejection
influence what I do or what I say,
especially when a group is involved?

Fans don't boo nobodies.
Baseball star REGGIE JACKSON

*[Jesus said,] "The Son of Man
must suffer much and be rejected."*

MARK 8:31

Early in his career, basketball superstar
Bill Russell was criticized for his style.
He says: "Before I came along
there were virtually no blocked shots
in the game of basketball. . . .
As late as my sophomore year in college,
my coach was telling me that my defensive
style was 'fundamentally unsound.' "
In a similar way, in Jesus' time, many
people considered Jesus' teachings ("love
your enemies") "fundamentally unsound."
Many people today still hold this opinion
of Jesus' teachings.

How seriously do I take such teachings
of Jesus as "love your enemies,
do good to those who hate you,
bless those who curse you,
and pray for those who mistreat you"
(LUKE 6:27-28)?

*If Jesus Christ were to come today,
people would not even crucify him.
They would ask him out to dinner,
and hear what he had to say,
and make fun of it.*

THOMAS CARLYLE

WEEK 24
Day 3

*[Jesus'] family . . .
set out to take charge of him,
because people were saying,
"He's gone mad!"*

MARK 3:21

In 1876, the president of Western Union laughed at Alexander Graham Bell, dubbing his telephone invention a useless "toy." In 1878, the British Parliament joked about Thomas Edison's plans for an electric light. In 1908, people ridiculed Billy Durant for suggesting that cars would someday replace the horse and buggy. In 1921, Tris Speaker criticized Babe Ruth, saying, "Ruth made a big mistake when he gave up pitching [and became an outfielder]." In 1940, military experts laughed at the suggestion that the helicopter had potential military value.

✓ As a rule, am I more prone
to speak up in praise or in blame?
Supportively or nonsupportively?
Constructively or destructively? Why?

*If a person calleth thee a donkey,
ignore that person.
If two persons calleth thee a donkey,
get thee a saddle.*

YIDDISH PROVERB

"Can anything good come from Nazareth?"
JOHN 1:46

One day a partially deaf boy came home
from school with a note from his teacher.
It suggested that he was too dull to learn
and was holding back the entire class.
When the boy's mother read it, she felt
terrible. But she also felt challenged.
"My son, Tom, is not too dull to learn,"
she said to herself. "I'll teach him
myself." When Tom died many years
later, the entire nation honored him in
a remarkable way. At exactly 9:59 P.M.,
Eastern Standard Time, every home in the
United States turned off its lights for
one minute, as a tribute to the man who had
invented those lights. Thomas Edison
invented not only the electric light but
also the movie projector and the record
player. When he died, the boy who was
"too dull to learn" had over a thousand
patents to his credit.

How much
do I let other people's negative remarks
discourage me?

He has the right to criticize
who has the heart to help.
ABRAHAM LINCOLN

WEEK 24
Day 5

Jesus said, "Forgive them, Father!
They don't know what they are doing."

LUKE 23:34

One of Hollywood's popular animated cartoon characters was a romantic skunk called Pepe LePew. He was forever falling in love with someone. But he was always rejected because of his odor. This didn't stop Pepe, however. He just kept right on loving—and right on being rejected. That's why filmgoers loved Pepe. He never gave up on people or on love. Pepe makes a beautiful image of Jesus. Jesus never gave up on people or on love either. He kept right on loving, no matter how many times he was rejected.

How do I respond
when people reject my attempts
to reach out to them in love?

Anyone can carry his burden,
however hard, until nightfall.
Anyone can do his work,
however hard, for one day.
Anyone can live sweetly,
patiently, lovingly, purely,
till the sun goes down.
And this is all that life really means.

ROBERT LOUIS STEVENSON

[Jesus] came to his own country,
but his own people did not receive him.

JOHN 1:11

One night a fisherman heard a splash.
A man on a nearby yacht had been
drinking and had fallen overboard. The
fisherman rescued him in the nick of time.
Next morning the fisherman returned to
see if the man was okay. "It's none of
your business," the man shouted. The
fisherman reminded him that he had
risked his own life to save him. Instead
of thanking the fisherman, the man
cursed him and told him to get out. The
fisherman said later: "I rowed away
with tears in my eyes. But the experience
was worth it, because it gave me
an understanding of how Jesus felt when
he was rejected by those he saved."

How able am I to draw good from bad?

I can say with complete truthfulness
that everything I have learned
in my seventy-five years in this world,
everything that has truly enhanced
and enlightened my experience,
has been through affliction
and not through happiness.

MALCOLM MUGGERIDGE

They picked up stones to throw at [Jesus].
JOHN 8:59

"If you can trust yourself when all men
doubt you, / But make allowance for their
doubting too . . . / Or being lied about,
don't deal in lies, / Or being hated, don't
give way to hating, . . . / If you can
dream—and not make dreams your master;
. . . / If you can meet with triumph and
disaster / And treat those two imposters
just the same; / If you can bear to hear
the truth you've spoken / Twisted by
knaves to make a trap for fools, / Or watch
the things you gave your life to broken, /
And stoop and build 'em up with wornout
tools; / If you can walk with crowds and
keep your virtue, / Or walk with kings—
nor lose the common touch; / If neither
foes nor loving friends can hurt you, / If
all men count with you, but none too
much; . . . / Yours is the Earth and
everything that's in it, / And—which is
more—you'll be a Man, my son!"
RUDYARD KIPLING, "If"

Reread the poem, pausing occasionally
to reflect on how it applied to Jesus.

Character is a victory, not a gift.
ANONYMOUS

WEEKLY MEETING
Sharing Agenda

1 On a scale of one (not at all) to ten (quite a bit), how much does fear of rejection influence me in what I say or do, for example, practice of my faith or defense of someone who is being bad-mouthed by a group?

2 How seriously do I take such teachings of Jesus as "love your enemies, do good to those who hate you, bless those who curse you, and pray for those who mistreat you"?

3 As a rule, am I more prone to be constructive or destructive in my criticism? Example?

4 How much do I let other people's negative remarks discourage me? Can I recall one such remark that hurt me quite a bit at the time?

5 How do I respond when people reject my attempts to reach out to them in love?

6 How able am I to draw good from bad experiences? Example?

7 What is my favorite line from Kipling's poem "If"? Why?

25 How well do I understand the Eucharist?

A church in Cologne, Germany, has a beautiful door containing four panels.

The first panel depicts six water jugs, symbols of the miracle of Cana, where Jesus changed water into wine.

The second panel depicts five loaves and two fish, symbols of the miracle near Capernaum, where Jesus multiplied bread and fish to feed a hungry crowd.

The third panel shows thirteen people at a table, symbolizing the Last Supper, where Jesus gave bread to his disciples, saying, "This is my body. . . . Do this in memory of me" (LUKE 22:19).

The fourth panel shows three people around a table, symbolizing the Emmaus supper on Easter Sunday night.

The door is a beautiful summary of the key teachings of the Bible concerning the Eucharist. It was—

- prefigured at Cana   Jn 2:1–11
- promised at Capernaum   Jn 6:24–59
- instituted at Jerusalem   Lk 22:14–20
- celebrated at Emmaus   Lk 24:13–35

This week's meditations focus on the incredible mystery of God's love as expressed in the Eucharist. The grace you ask for is:

Father, bless me with the grace
to enter into the heart of your Son,
that I might better understand
how the Eucharist
expresses your love for me and
why Jesus said,
"Do this in memory of me."

Weekly Instruction

This week you may wish to celebrate the Eucharist on one or several mornings.

As always, this is only a suggestion. The important thing is to be attentive to anything the Holy Spirit may prompt you to consider or do.

Daily Reading

1	Eucharist prefigured	Jn 2:1–11
2	Eucharist promised	Jn 6:24–51
3	Eucharist instituted	Lk 22:14–20
4	Eucharist celebrated	Lk 24:13–35
5	Eucharist: hard saying	Jn 6:52–59
6	Eucharist: oneness	1 Cor 10:16–17
7	Eucharist: Lord's Supper	1 Cor 11:17–34

WEEK 25
Day 1 _____

The day before the Passover . . .
Jesus knew that the hour had come. . . .
[And so when all were seated for the
Passover meal, Jesus] rose . . .
and began to wash the disciples' feet.

JOHN 13:1, 4-5

Richard Foster writes:
"The disciples [knew] . . . that someone
needed to wash the others' feet.
The problem was that the only people
who washed feet were the least. . . .
It was such a sore point that
they were not even going to talk about it.
Then Jesus took a towel and basin
and redefined greatness."
The disciples were deeply moved. Jesus
said to them, "I have set an example for
you, so that you will do just what I have
done" (JOHN 13:15).

What does Jesus' example say to me, and
how does it apply to my life right now?

[Jesus said,] "If you are about to offer
your gift to God at the altar
and there you remember that your brother
[or sister] has something against you, . . .
go at once and make peace . . . and then
come back and offer your gift to God."

MATTHEW 5:23-24

[Jesus said,] "Take this and share it."
LUKE 22:17

Jesus introduced the Passover meal in the traditional way. He prepared a cup of red wine, saying, "Take this and share it." Sharing the same cup dramatized the unity of all present. Red wine recalled both the blood-marked doors in Egypt and the covenant blood at Mount Sinai. The meal traditionally began with the eating of bitter herbs. This was the cue for the youngest to ask, "Why is this meal different?" The father then explained the meaning attached to the foods to be eaten: The *bitter herbs* recalled Israel's years of bitter slavery in Egypt. The *unleavened bread* recalled Israel's swift exit from Egypt—not even waiting for the next day's bread to rise. The *lamb* recalled God's instructions to the Israelite families to *sacrifice a lamb* and eat its flesh (EXODUS 12).

When I imagine myself sitting at the table with the disciples and listening to Jesus, what strikes me about his explanation of the foods, especially the lamb?

We are nobly born. Fortunate those who know it; blessed those who remember it.
ROBERT LOUIS STEVENSON

WEEK 25
Day 3

[Jesus said,] "Do this in memory of me."
                                    LUKE 22:19

After the eating of the herbs came the
"breaking of bread." A reverent silence
fell upon the disciples as Jesus took bread
in his weather-beatened hands, gave
thanks, and said to them,
"Take this and share it among yourselves.
This is my body, which is given for you.
Do this in memory of me" (LUKE 22:17, 19).
The disciples were struck by Jesus' words
over the bread: "This is my body." They
recalled the day in the synagogue at
Capernaum when Jesus proclaimed,
"I am the living bread that came down
from heaven. If anyone eats this bread,
he will live forever.
The bread that I will give . . .
is my flesh, which I give
so that the world may live" (JOHN 6:51).
After Jesus spoke these words, many of
his disciples would no longer walk with
him (JOHN 6:66).

Why do I continue to walk with Jesus
in spite of what he said at Capernaum?

The bread we break: when we eat it,
we are sharing in the body of Christ.
                              1 CORINTHIANS 10:16

[Then Jesus said,] "This is my blood."
MARK 14:24

Jesus ended the Passover meal in the
traditional way. He prepared a final cup
of wine. Holding it up, he said,
"This cup is God's new covenant
sealed with my blood,
which is poured out for you" (LUKE 22:20).
Jesus' reference to a *new* covenant recalled
God's promise to Jeremiah:
"The time is coming
when I will make a new covenant
with the people of Israel" (JEREMIAH 31:31).
The disciples would have been struck by
Jesus' reference to his blood being poured
out. It recalled the old covenant, when
Moses poured blood on the people, saying,
"This is the blood that seals the covenant
which the LORD made with you" (EXODUS 24:8).
The disciples must have sensed that
something marvelous was taking place.

What do I sense as I imagine myself sitting
across from Jesus during this episode?

The cup we use in the Lord's Supper
and for which we give thanks to God:
when we drink from it,
we are sharing in the blood of Christ.
1 CORINTHIANS 10:16

[Jesus took bread,]
gave thanks to God, broke it, and said,
"This is my body, which is for you.
Do this in memory of me."

1 CORINTHIANS 11:23-24

A man turned his life around. When asked
how he did it, he took from his wallet a
photo of a caseworker, saying, "When I'm
tempted to return to my old ways, I
remember what this person did for me,
and I draw strength from that memory."
The Eucharist performs a similar role for
us. We remember what Jesus did for us
and draw strength from that memory.
But the Eucharist does infinitely more.
For Jews, to *remember* a religious event
meant more than to recall it. It meant to
bring it into the present by faith and to
receive from it the same blessing that
those originally present received. This is
the meaning that Jesus had in mind when
he said, "Do this in memory of me."

How do I respond to Jesus' request?

[The memory is] a spacious country
of the mind, wherein a thousand saints,
artists, musicians, and lovers . . .
live, speak, teach, carve, and sing.

WILL DURANT

I will not die; instead I will live.
PSALM 118:17

After the Passover meal, Jesus and his
disciples sang the Hallel. No doubt tears
flooded their eyes as they did. Jews had
been singing it now for over a thousand
years. Its words read:
"I am your servant, LORD. . . .
I will give you what I have promised. . . .
I will not die; instead, I will live
and proclaim what the LORD has done. . . .
The stone
which the builders rejected as worthless
turned out to be the most important of all.
This was done by the LORD;
what a wonderful sight it is!
This is the day of the LORD's victory;
let us be happy, let us celebrate!"
PSALM 116:16, 19; 118:17, 22-24

What phrase of the Hallel strikes me most
as I reread it slowly and reverently,
meditating on how it applies
in a special way to Jesus
as he began his final hours on earth?

Thy praise shall sound
from shore to shore,
Till suns shall rise and set no more.
ISAAC WATTS

WEEK 25
Day 7 _____

Every time you eat this bread
and drink from this cup,
you proclaim the Lord's death
until he comes.

1 CORINTHIANS 11:26

Mark ends his account of the Last Supper,
saying, "Then they sang a hymn and
went out to the Mount of Olives" (MARK 14:26).
The disciples felt a deep joy as they
walked along under the stars. But it would
have been bittersweet, for Jesus had said
too many sorrow-tinged things. For
example, he said, "This is my body, which
is given for you. . . . [This is] my blood,
which is poured out for you" (LUKE 22:19-20).
Even though Jesus had warned his disciples
that he was to die violently (MATTHEW 16:21),
they never quite got the point. Nor did
they get it now.

In what sense is my experience at the
Eucharist a bittersweet joy—as was the
disciples' joy at the Last Supper?

Every time ministers call their people
around the table, they call them
to experience not only the Lord's presence
but his absence as well; they call them
to . . . sadness as well as to joy.

HENRI J. M. NOUWEN

WEEKLY MEETING
Sharing Agenda

1 What example did Jesus set by washing the disciples' feet before the Last Supper? How might it have a message for me right now?

2 What struck me most as I imagined sitting at table and listening to Jesus explain the meaning of the foods, especially the lamb?

3 Why do I continue to walk with Jesus in the Eucharist or Mass, even though many people no longer do so?

4 What struck me most as I imagined sitting at table across from Jesus as he took the cup of wine and prayed over it?

5 How might I explain to Jesus my apathy and the apathy of others to his request, "Do this in memory of me"?

6 What phrase of the Hallel struck me most as I reread it and meditated on how it applied to Jesus as he began the last day of his life on earth?

7 In what sense is the Eucharist today still a bittersweet joy—as was the Last Supper?

26 How well do I appreciate the Eucharist?

Some years ago, Catholics did not eat or drink anything for twenty-four hours before receiving Communion. During this era Father Walter Ciszek was arrested by the Russians and falsely accused of being a "Vatican spy."

Ciszek spent the next twenty-three years in prisons and labor camps. After his release he wrote a book about his ordeal. In one passage Ciszek describes how precious the Eucharist was to prisoners. They would rise early and celebrate it in secret, knowing they would be severely punished if caught. This made it hard for many prisoners to participate. Ciszek writes in *He Leadeth Me:*

"We would consecrate extra bread
and distribute Communion
to the other prisoners when we could.
Sometimes that meant we would
only see them when we returned
to the barracks at night for dinner.
Yet these men would actually fast
all day long and do exhausting
physical labor without a bite to eat
since the evening before, just to be able
to receive the Holy Eucharist."

This week's meditations focus on the incredible mystery of God's love as expressed in the Eucharist. The grace you ask for is:

Father, bless me with the grace
to enter into the heart of your Son,
that I might better appreciate
how the Eucharist
expresses your love for me and
why Jesus said,
"Do this in memory of me."

Weekly Instruction

Once again, you may feel moved to celebrate the Eucharist on one or several occasions during the week. Don't feel obligated to do this; simply keep your heart open to the possibility that the Holy Spirit may move you to want to do this.

Daily Reading

1	Lord's disciples	Jn 12:12-19
2	Lord's body	1 Cor 12:12-27
3	Lord's presence	Ex 33:7-10
4	Lord's bread	Jn 6:41-52
5	Lord's light	Mt 5:14-16
6	Lord's command	Lk 6:7-36
7	Lord's peace	Jn 20:19-21

WEEK 26
Day 1 _____

*[Jesus said,] "What Moses gave you was not
the bread from heaven; it is my Father
who gives you the real bread. . . .
I am the living bread that came down
from heaven. If anyone eats this bread,
he will live forever."*

JOHN 6:32, 51

Each year Catholics celebrate the feast of
the Body of Christ. Sometimes it includes
an outdoor procession. Here is how an
African bishop describes such a procession
during a rain storm in Nigeria in 1986.
"The people danced and sang in the rain.
It was the first time I recall the Blessed
Sacrament being carried . . . to the sound
of . . . cheering and clapping. Everyone
was drenched. No one thought of seeking
shelter or running away. Judges, lawyers,
doctors, mothers, children stood their
ground as if nothing was happening
except the Eucharist. I have not seen
anything like it here or anywhere else."
America magazine

Would I have stayed in that procession
to honor the Body of Christ? Why?

*Jesus cannot be our Savior
unless he is first our Lord.*

HUGH C. BURR

All of us . . . are one body,
for we all share the same loaf.

1 CORINTHIANS 10:17

Astronauts Aldrin and Armstrong had
just landed on the moon. While Armstrong
prepared for his moon walk, Aldrin
unpacked bread and wine. Aldrin writes:
"I poured the wine into the chalice. . . .
In the one-sixth gravity of the moon
the wine curled slowly and gracefully
up the side of the cup. It was interesting
to think that the very first liquid
ever poured on the moon
and the very first food eaten there
were communion elements." He adds,
"I sensed especially strong my unity
with our church back home, and the Church
everywhere." *Guideposts Treasury of Hope*

What is one thing I might do to develop
a stronger sense of unity with
other Christians, locally and globally?

In Jesus Christ,
true God and true man . . .
rests our hope for real humanity.
Not by ourselves,
but insofar as we are members
of the Body of Christ.

KARL BARTH

WEEK 26
Day 3 _____

"My Lord and my God!"
JOHN 20:28

Steve Garwood brought the Body of Christ
home to his wife, who was still recuperating
from childbirth. Some friends were there
to see the new baby. So he placed the pyx
containing the Body of Christ on a shelf
in the living room. Visitors streamed in
all day. By the time the last one left, Steve
had not yet had time to be alone with his
wife, who had just fallen asleep. As he
passed through the darkened living room
on his way to bed, Steve felt compelled to
kneel down before the Body of Christ. As
he bowed his head, he was struck by the
fact that he was not alone. The Lord was
there. This realization totally overwhelmed
him. He said later,
"Blood pounded in my ears
and all the hairs of my body stood on end.
I prayed, 'Lord Jesus Christ, Son of God,
have mercy on me.' "

Can I recall a time when
the realization of the divine presence
totally—or greatly—overwhelmed me?

*The LORD your God, who is present
with you, is a great and awesome God.*
DEUTERONOMY 7:21 (NRSV)

Has anyone had this experience

[Jesus said,] "Where two or three
come together in my name,
I am there with them."

MATTHEW 18:20

A religious persecution in 1980 left a
region of Guatemala without priests. But
the people continued to meet in their
churches. Once a month they sent delegates
to a part of Guatemala where priests still
functioned. Traveling up to eighteen hours
on foot, the delegates put a basket of bread
on the altar and celebrated the Eucharist
in the name of their parish. After the
Mass they took the bread home. Now it
was the Body of Christ. When the
government threatened to close all
churches, the people said,
"If the authorities forbid us to meet
in the churches, we shall gather
under the trees of the wood or
in the caves of the mountains."

FERNANDO BERMUDEZ,
Death and Resurrection in Guatemala

Why do I celebrate the Eucharist?

Jesus said . . . "If you do not eat the flesh
of the Son of Man and drink his blood,
you will not have life in yourselves."

JOHN 6:53

WEEK 26
Day 5 _____

You are Christ's body,
and each one is a part of it.
1 CORINTHIANS 12:27

William Barclay tells the story of an old
African chief of the Ngoni tribe. One
Sunday morning he sat at the Eucharist,
watching members of the Ngoni, Senga,
and Tumbuka tribes worshiping side by
side. Suddenly his mind flashed back to
his boyhood, and he recalled watching
Ngoni warriors, after a day's fighting,
washing Senga and Tumbuka blood from
their spears and bodies. That morning at
the Eucharist, the old chief understood
as never before what Christianity is all
about. It is God, calling all people in and
through Christ to put away all hostility
and live as one family. This is the message
the Christian community proclaims to the
world each time it gathers to celebrate the
Eucharist.

How important is my presence
at the Eucharist on the Lord's Day?

The Christian community is Christ's body.
If it is silent, Christ is silent.
If I am silent, a part of Christ is silent.
If a part of Christ is silent,
a part of Christ's message goes unheard.

Christ himself has brought us peace.
EPHESIANS 2:14

Some members of the French underground were arrested by the German army and sentenced to death by firing squad. On the eve of their execution, the prisoners, mostly Catholic, asked to celebrate the Eucharist. The Germans explained that the only priest available was German. After discussing the matter, the prisoners agreed to accept the priest. Now, one of the German guards happened to be Catholic also. He asked to join the French prisoners at Mass. In such a situation one might question whether it was possible for the prisoners to allow the guard to share the Eucharist with them. After discussing the matter, the prisoners said to the guard, "Leave your rifle outside the door if you wish to join us."

If I had been one of the prisoners at the Mass, what would I have thought as I turned to the German guard and extended the handshake of peace to him?

Lord,
make me an instrument of your peace;
where there is hatred, let me sow love.
SAINT FRANCIS OF ASSISI

WEEK 26
Day 7 _____

[Jesus said,] "Peace be with you."
JOHN 20:19

The "eye" of a hurricane is an amazing
thing. To get an idea of it, picture a
Frisbee with a small hole cut out of its
center. Expand the Frisbee until its
diameter measures a hundred miles across
and the hole's diameter measures ten
miles across. Now, spin the Frisbee at the
rate of one hundred miles per hour. That's
what a hurricane is like. But keep in mind
that inside the "eye" of the hurricane
there is no wind, only blue skies and a
shining sun. The hurricane's "eye" is an
image of the Eucharist. Political storms
may rage about us, but in the Eucharist
there is a peaceful calm, blue skies of hope,
and a shining "Son." But Jesus never
intended that we remain in the eucharistic
"eye." We are to go back into the storm
and become an "eye" of peace to others.
We are to share with them the peace that
Jesus shared with us.

How might I best share with others
the peace Jesus has shared with me?

*"Happy are those who work for peace;
God will call them his children!"*
MATTHEW 5:9

WEEKLY MEETING
Sharing Agenda

1 Why would I have continued to march in the procession in Nigeria during a rain storm to honor the Body of Christ?

2 What is one thing I might do to develop a stronger sense of unity with other Christians, locally and globally?

3 Can I recall a time when the realization of the divine presence totally—or greatly—overwhelmed me?

4 Why do I celebrate the Eucharist?

5 How important is my presence at the Eucharist on the Lord's Day?

6 As I imagined that I was one of the prisoners at the Mass, what were my thoughts as I turned to the German guard and extended the handshake of peace to him?

7 How might I best share with others the peace Jesus has shared with me?

27 How ready am I to say yes to God's will?

There was no radar to guide artillery shells in World War I. Missiles were simply lobbed over hills and trees much as one lobs a rock over a brick wall at some hidden target.

To remedy this situation, artillery officers used to go aloft in hot-air balloons to locate the target and give directions to their gunners.

Going up in the balloon was a dangerous job, because the person was a perfect target. One officer said that just the thought of going up made him "sweat blood." We can all relate to how that officer felt. We too have had to do things we dreaded.

Jesus was no exception. He also had to do things he dreaded. One of them was facing the ordeal that lay ahead of him on Good Friday.

This week's meditations focus on Jesus' agony in the Garden of Gethsemane, when Jesus actually "sweat blood" over what the next day would bring (see LUKE 22:44). The grace you ask for is:

Lord,
touch my heart with compassion
for all that Jesus suffered for me
that I may be moved to say yes
to all that he may ask of me.

Weekly Instruction

In your meditations this week, you might
keep in mind the words of Atticus Finch
in the novel *To Kill a Mockingbird*. He tells
his children that if you want to understand
another person, you must crawl inside
that person's skin and walk around with
him or her. You might try to use this
approach as you meditate on the sufferings
of Jesus this week.

Keep in mind, also, that meditating on the
sufferings of Jesus has probably started
more people on the road to sanctity than
any other form of prayer.

Daily Reading

1	Prophecy of Jesus	Mk 14:27–31
2	Agony of Jesus	Mk 14:32–34
3	Prayer of Jesus	Mk 14:32–42
4	Betrayal of Jesus	Lk 22:47–53
5	Arrest of Jesus	Mk 14:43–51
6	Power of Jesus	Jn 18:1–7
7	Taking of Jesus	Jn 18:12–14

WEEK 27
Day 1 _____

Anguish came over [Jesus], and he said . . .
"The sorrow in my heart is so great
that it almost crushes me."

MARK 14:33–34

John Powell's book *He Touched Me* came
from the heart. After John finished it, he
felt uneasy about what he had written.
So he ended the book with these words:
"Some of the admissions . . .
in these pages . . . come hard for me. . . .
And I hope you will accept [them] . . .
the way I have intended [them] . . .
as an act of love."
After the book was published, John received
four to five letters a week from people,
thanking him for sharing with them his
vulnerability. Jesus does something similar
in Gethsemane. He shares his vulnerability
with us. And instead of making him less
attractive, it makes him more attractive.

If sharing my vulnerability
has such a beneficial impact on others
and makes me more attractive to them,
why don't I share it, as Jesus did?

Our High Priest . . . [can] feel sympathy
for our weaknesses. . . . [He] was tempted
in every way that we are, but did not sin.

HEBREWS 4:15

[Jesus left his disciples. He went off alone,]
knelt down and prayed. "Father," he said,
"if you will, take this cup of suffering
away from me. Not my will, however,
but your will be done."

LUKE 22:41-42

Robert Granat's short story "The Sign"
concerns a young man named Davidson.
He has just mailed his first novel to a
publishing house. Filled with fear about
the publisher's decision, he goes outside
and paces back and forth in an orchard.
It was Holy Week, and his thoughts
seesawed back and forth to Christ in the
garden and "to himself in the orchard . . .
to Christ preparing for the supreme agony
of hanging by nails . . . to himself and his
book with Dow Press. . . . He stopped and
said . . . 'Thy will, not mine.' " Then it
hit him. He really meant, "God, let your
will coincide with mine and let things
work out to the glory of each of us." Then
Davidson sat down and cried.

Can I recall a time when I found myself
in Davidson's situation?

The Will of God—
Nothing More, Nothing Less.
Motto of G. CAMPBELL MORGAN

WEEK 27
Day 3 _____

Once more Jesus . . . prayed,
"My Father, ... your will be done."

MATTHEW 26:42

Catherine Marshall was critically ill. No
amount of medicine and prayer helped.
One day she read about a missionary who
had been in a similar situation. The
missionary finally resigned herself to
God's will, saying, "Lord, I give up!"
Within weeks, she recovered. Catherine
thought the story strange. But she could
not forget it. Finally, she too resigned
herself to God's will, saying, "I'm tired of
asking. You decide what you want for
me!" And the result? Catherine says,
"It was as if I had touched a button. . . .
From that moment my recovery began."

What might the stories of the two women
be saying to me right now?

✳ *How often we look upon God*
as our last and feeblest response!
We go to [God]
because we have nowhere else to go.
And then we learn
that the storms of life have driven us
not upon the rocks,
but into the desired haven.

GEORGE MacDONALD

Again Jesus . . . went away,
and prayed the third time,
saying the same words.

MATTHEW 26:44

British essayist Gilbert K. Chesterton
has written:
"In everything worth having,
even in every pleasure,
there is a point of pain or tedium
that must be survived. . . .
The joy of the battle comes
after the first fear. . . .
The joy of reading Virgil comes
after the bore of learning him;
the glow of the sea bather comes
after the shock of the sea bath;
and the success of marriage comes
after the failure of the honeymoon."
It is the same
with learning and doing God's will.
The peace comes only after the pain
of facing possible defeat—
as Jesus experienced in Gethsemane.

Can I recall a time when I nearly gave up
because of the initial pain involved?

Character consists of what you do
on the third and fourth tries.

JAMES MICHENER

WEEK 27
Day 5 —————————————————

*[When the soldiers announced
that they had come
to arrest Jesus of Nazareth,
Jesus said,]* "I am he."
*[At Jesus' reply, the soldiers]
fell to the ground.*

JOHN 18:5-6

A modern commentator says of this
unusual episode:
"It may well be that in this instance,
the guards suddenly felt
the full force of Jesus' personality
and were utterly dismayed. . . . In any case
it is obvious . . . that John intends
to picture it as miraculous,
thereby emphasizing the perfect freedom
with which Jesus accepted arrest."

GUISEPPE RICCIOTTI

Do I know of anyone who seems to radiate
"power" just by his or her presence?
How do I explain it?

*Jesus and all the genuine saints
throughout history had spiritual power and
they had a deep prayer life.
We believe that there must be
some connection between
their power and their prayer life.*

SHERWOOD EDDY

[Jesus said to the soldiers,]
"If . . . you are looking for me,
let these others go."

JOHN 18:8

Ernie Pyle was a newspaper columnist
who lived in the trenches with the soldiers
in World War II. He jotted down in a
notebook what he heard them say. For
example, one young man said,
"I'm fighting hard, Mr. Pyle,
but it's hell out here. At times,
when the big guns get whaling away,
when snipers start poppin'
from the hedges,
I just want to fold my tent."

Because Jesus had a human heart,
he experienced human fear, as we do.
Yet, after embracing his Father's will,
he showed incredible courage. Why?
Can I recall an experience of courage
after I chose to embrace God's will?

We shall steer safely
through every storm,
so long as our heart is right,
our intention is fervent,
our courage is steadfast, and
our trust is fixed firmly on God.
SAINT FRANCIS DE SALES

WEEK 27
Day 7 _____

*[Peter took a sword to defend Jesus, but
Jesus said,] "Put your sword back. . . .
Do you think that I will not
drink the cup of suffering
which my Father has given me?"*

JOHN 18:11

William Barclay draws a fascinating
comparison between the Jesus who entered
the garden and the Jesus who left it.
He writes in *The Gospel of Luke:*
"A famous pianist said
of Chopin's nocturne in C-sharp minor,
'I must tell you about it. . . .
In this piece all is sorrow and trouble
. . . until he begins to speak to God,
to pray; then it is all right.'
That is the way it was with Jesus.
He went into Gethsemane in the dark;
he came out in the light—
because he talked with God.
He went into Gethsemane in agony;
he came out with peace in his soul—
because he talked with God."

Can I recall a time when I began prayer
in agony and concluded it in peace?

*Prayer does not change God,
but changes him who prays.*
SOREN KIERKEGAARD

WEEKLY MEETING
Sharing Agenda

1 If sharing my vulnerability has such a positive impact on others and makes me more attractive to them, why am I so reluctant to share it with them when I experience it, as Jesus did?

2 What is the biggest thing that keeps me from saying, right now, "Not my will, Lord, but your will be done"?

3 How do I explain what happened to the missionary and to Catherine Marshall? What might their stories be saying to me at this very moment?

4 Can I recall a time when I nearly gave up because of the initial pain involved? What kept me going?

5 Do I know of anyone who seems to radiate a "power" just by his or her presence? How do I explain it?

6 Can I recall a time when I experienced an influx of courage after I chose to embrace God's will? How do I explain it?

7 Can I recall a time when I began my prayer in darkness and ended it in light? Began it in agony and ended it in peace?

28 How ready am I to suffer for Jesus as he did for me?

Albrecht Durer was a famous sixteenth-century German painter. One of his masterpieces is called *Descent from the Cross*.

A moving detail in the painting shows a disciple holding Jesus' crown of thorns and pressing his finger against it to see how much pain Jesus had felt.

This week's meditations focus on the sufferings of Jesus. Their purpose is to lead to a deeper knowledge, love, and service of him. The grace you ask for is:

Father,
give me a deeper insight
into why Jesus suffered for me
that I may be moved to say yes
more lovingly and joyfully
to whatever Jesus may ask of me.

Weekly Instruction

This week you may feel moved to pray the Stations of the Cross. The procedure is simply to contemplate for a half minute or so on each of the "stations" listed on the next page. In other words, imagine that you are present in person at each station. You hear what Jesus heard, see what he saw, and feel what he felt.

1 Jesus is condemned to death.
2 Jesus carries his cross.
3 Jesus falls the first time.
4 Jesus meets his mother.
5 Jesus is helped by Simon.
6 Jesus' face is wiped by Veronica.
7 Jesus falls a second time.
8 Jesus speaks to the women.
9 Jesus falls a third time.
10 Jesus is stripped of his clothes.
11 Jesus is nailed to the cross.
12 Jesus dies.
13 Jesus is taken down from the cross.
14 Jesus is laid in the tomb.

Daily Reading

1 Jesus is interrogated   Mk 14:53-56
2 Jesus identifies himself   Mk 14:57-62
3 Jesus is accused   Mk 14:63-65
4 Peter denies Jesus   Mk 14:66-72
5 Jesus before Pilate   Mk 15:1-5
6 Jesus is condemned   Mk 15:6-15
7 Jesus is ridiculed   Mt 15:16-20

WEEK 28
Day 1

*[The soldiers led Jesus from Gethsemane
to the house of the High Priest.
Later, Peter showed up at the house and
was accused of being a disciple.
Peter vehemently denied it three times,
as Jesus had foretold.
Then, Peter] went out and wept bitterly.*

MATTHEW 26:75

Peter's panic-stricken denials recall a
scene from the novel *Lord Jim*. As a boy,
Jim spent hours dreaming of doing brave
deeds at sea. Eventually he grew up and
became the skipper of the *Patna*. One night
the *Patna* struck something and began to
sink. In a fit of unexplainable panic, Jim
leaped into the sea to save himself.
Although braver hands saved the ship and
its passengers, Jim never forgave himself.
Years later, however, he bought back his
salvation with a splendid act of courage
that exceeded his wildest boyhood dreams.

Can I recall a moment of weakness,
when I did something similar
to what Peter or Jim did?
What kind of an impact did it have
on my life—for good or ill?

*A weakness can, with God's help,
become the strongest thing about us.*

*[They took Jesus to Pilate, who tried
to set Jesus free, but the crowd shouted,]*
"Crucify him! Crucify him!"

LUKE 23:21

A famous troupe of actors was going to
dramatize the crucifixion of Jesus. They
invited local people to make up the crowd
scene. A little boy was chosen by members
of his class to represent them. For a week
he looked forward to being on stage with
real actors. Just before curtain time, the
director introduced the local people to
their "leaders," saying, "Do and shout
exactly what they do!" Then the curtain
went up. On a balcony at center stage
stood Jesus and Pilate. The "leaders"
began shaking their fists at Jesus and
shouting to Pilate, "Crucify him! Crucify
him!" The townspeople did the same—all
but the boy. Try as he may, he could not
bring himself to shake his fist at Jesus and
shout, "Crucify him!" Instead, he began
to cry for Jesus.

What feelings do I have
when I put myself in the boy's shoes?

Go not where a path happens to be.
Go rather where a path ought to be.

ANONYMOUS

X

WEEK 28
Day 3 ─────────────────

Pilate took Jesus and had him whipped.
JOHN 19:1

During Holy Week of 1986, *USA Today* carried a story about Jesus' crucifixion. It was based on an article by a doctor in the *New England Journal of Medicine.* The doctor said Christians tend to romanticize the death of Jesus. In reality, it was brutal beyond belief. Ancient writers tell us that whippings often preceded the crucifixion and that victims sometimes died before the whipping was over. They also tell us that crucifixion victims sometimes went insane. One writer says that after the fall of Jerusalem in A.D. 70, Jewish freedom fighters waged guerrilla warfare against the Romans. One day the leader of a guerrilla group was captured. When the Romans prepared to crucify him, the others surrendered rather than see their leader suffer such a horrible execution.

What keeps me from offering
my day-to-day sufferings to Jesus
in reparation for his sufferings or
to win God's grace
to complete Jesus' work?

Z *When you get the damned hurt—use it.*
ERNEST HEMINGWAY

*They stripped off his clothes
and put a scarlet robe on him.
Then they made a crown
out of thorny branches
and placed it on his head.*

MATTHEW 27:28-29

In *Deliver Us from Evil*, Dr. Tom Dooley
tells about treating an old priest who was
punished by the Communists in southeast
Asia for "preaching treason." Eight nails
were driven into his head: three in the
front, two in the back, and three across
the top. Dooley writes:
"I washed the scalp, dislodged the clots,
and opened the pockets to let the pus
escape. I gave the priest massive doses
of penicillin and tetanous oxide. . . .
The old man pulled through.
One day when I went to treat him,
he had disappeared. Fr. Lopez told me
that he had gone back . . .
behind the Bamboo Curtain. This meant
he had gone back to his torturers."

Why would the old priest go back again?
What would motivate me to go back?

*It is the crushed grape
that yields the wine.*

ANONYMOUS

They spat in his face and beat him.

MATTHEW 26:67

Flannery O'Connor wrote a short story
called "Parker's Back." It's about a man
named Parker, who lives with his wife,
Sarah Ruth, in a poor shack in the deep
South. She constantly badgers him about
his lack of religion. She also despises the
tattoos that checker his body. Determined
to please her, just once, Parker decides to
have a tattoo of Jesus needled on his back.
When Sarah Ruth sees it, she shouts,
"Idolatry!" Then she grabs a blunt
instrument and begins beating him
savagely across his back. He was so
stunned, he just "sat there and let her
beat him, until she nearly knocked him
senseless and large welts had formed on
the face of the tattooed Christ."

Can I recall a time
when I accepted another's abuse
rather than make matters worse?
Can I recall ever doing so
simply to be more like Christ?

Christ himself carried our sins
in his body to the cross. . . . It is
by his wounds that you have been healed.

1 PETER 2:24

*Pilate went back out once more
and said to the crowd,
"Look, I will bring him out here to you
to let you see that I cannot find
any reason to condemn him."
So Jesus came out. . . .
When the chief priests
and the Temple guards saw him,
they shouted,
"Crucify him! Crucify him!"*

JOHN 19:4-6

C. E. Montague's novel *Rough Justice*
describes a little boy sitting in church
with his mother. His mouth and his eyes
are wide open. The boy is listening for the
first time to the story of the crucifixion
of Jesus. He is so deeply moved by what
he hears that he begins to sob somewhat
audibly. When people turn around and
look at the boy, his mother bends down
over him and whispers cheerily, "Honey,
you shouldn't take the story so seriously!"

In what way might I be like the mother
of the boy in Montague's novel? Why?

*It might take a crucified church
to bring a crucified Christ
before the eyes of the world.*
W. E. ORCHARD

WEEK 28
Day 7 _____

[Pilate] handed him over to be crucified.

MARK 15:15

Father Titus Brandsma was arrested and taken to a Nazi concentration camp. There he was put in an old dog kennel. His guards amused themselves by ordering him to bark like a dog each time they passed. Eventually the priest died from torture. What the Nazis didn't know was that he had recorded his ordeal between the lines of print in an old prayerbook. One page contains this poem to Jesus:

"No grief shall fall my way, but I
Shall see your grief-filled eyes;
The lonely way that you once walked
Has made me sorrow-wise. . . .
Thy love has turned to brightest light
This night-like way. . . .
Stay with me, Lord, only stay;
I shall not fear
If, reaching out my hand,
I feel Thee near."

When I reread the poem in a whisper, speaking it directly to Jesus as I look into his face, what does he say to me?

*If ever man was God or God man,
Jesus Christ was both.*

GEORGE GORDON, LORD BYRON

WEEKLY MEETING
Sharing Agenda

1 Can I recall a weak moment when I did something similar to what Peter or Jim in the novel *Lord Jim* did? How did it impact my life for good or ill?

2 Did putting myself in the shoes of the little boy (told to shake his fist and shout, "Crucify him!") help or hinder my prayer? How?

3 What keeps me from offering my day-to-day sufferings to Jesus in reparation for his sufferings or to win God's grace to complete Jesus' work?

4 Why would the old priest described by Tom Dooley go behind the Bamboo Curtain again? What might motivate me to go back if I were the priest?

5 Can I recall a time when I accepted another's abuse rather than make matters worse? Can I recall ever doing so simply to be more like Christ?

6 To what extent am I like the mother of the boy (listening to the crucifixion story for the first time)? Why?

7 When I reread Father Brandsma's poem in a whisper, speaking it while looking into Jesus' face, what impact did it have? What did Jesus say to me?

29 How ready am I to die for Jesus as he died for me?

The science-fiction story "The Traveler" is about a scientist named Paul Jairus. He's part of a research team that has invented an energy screen that makes it possible to travel backward into time.

Jairus is picked to make the first flight. He decides to fly back to the crucifixion of Jesus. Jairus is a nonbeliever and anticipates finding it quite different from the way the Bible describes it.

At the appointed moment, Jairus finds himself soaring backward into history. Minutes later the energy screen touches down on target. The crucifixion site is swarming with people.

Jairus asks the Command Center to allow him to move closer to the cross. They grant it but warn him to stay inside the energy screen. Suddenly something unexpected happens. Jairus feels drawn to Jesus. He is deeply moved by the love radiating from Jesus. It's something he never experienced before.

Then, contrary to all his expectations, the events of the crucifixion unfold exactly as the gospel describes them. Jairus is visibly shaken. The Command Center realizes this and tells him to return to the twentieth century immediately. Jairus protests, but to no avail. When Jairus steps from the energy screen, he is a changed man.

This week's meditations focus on the crucifixion of Jesus. It is hoped that what happened to Jairus will happen to you. The grace you ask for is:

Lord, touch my heart with compassion
for what Jesus suffered for me
that I may say yes to what he may ask of me.

Weekly Instruction

This week you may find it helpful to keep a crucifix before you. Consider ending each meditation by kissing the five wounds of Jesus: his pierced hands, his pierced feet, and his pierced side.

Daily Reading

1	Weep not for me	Lk 23:26–31
2	Come down if you can	Mt 27:33–44
3	Forgive them, Father	Lk 23:32–34
4	Remember me, Jesus	Lk 23:40–43
5	Death of Jesus	Mt 27:45–50
6	Act of faith in Jesus	Mt 27:51–55
7	Burial of Jesus	Mt 27:57–66

WEEK 29
Day 1

The soldiers led Jesus away. . . .
A large crowd of people followed him;
among them were some women
who were weeping and wailing.

LUKE 23:26-27

A Good Friday procession trailed along
an inner-city street in Chicago. Leading
it was a man carrying a heavy eight-foot
cross. Behind him walked other men in
baseball caps and leather jackets. They
were carrying smaller crosses. People
came out of rundown buildings and
spontaneously joined the procession.
Occasionally the marchers paused at a
place of pain—an alleged crack house, a
spot where a boy was shot. At one point
a woman ran up and hugged the man with
the large cross; at another point a youth
offered to help him carry it.

What goes on inside me as I see people
spontaneously joining the marchers?

The Way of the Cross
winds through our towns. . . .
It takes the road of poverty and suffering
in every form.
It is in front of these new Stations . . .
that we must stop and meditate.

MICHAEL QUOIST, *Prayers of Life*

*When they came
to the place called "The Skull,"
they crucified Jesus there.*

LUKE 23:33

A priest was speaking to students at a
school for the deaf. As an interpreter
translated his words into sign language,
the priest noticed that she frequently
touched her fingers to the palms of her
hands. He learned later that this was the
sign for "Jesus," whose palms were nailed
to the cross.

When I am in pain,
how helpful is it to recall
that Jesus suffered terribly
and understands what I am enduring?

*I carry a cross in my pocket. . . .
It's not for . . . the world to see.
It's simply an understanding
Between my Savior and me. . . .
It reminds me to be thankful
For my blessings day by day
And strive to serve him better
In all that I do and say. . . .
Reminding no one but me
That Jesus Christ is Lord of my life
If only I'll let him be.*

ANONYMOUS

WEEK 29
Day 3 _____

[Hanging in pain on the cross,]
Jesus said, "Forgive them, Father!
They don't know what they are doing."

LUKE 23:34

In his novel *Legion,* William Blatty portrays
a Jewish detective standing all alone in a
church. A priest had just been murdered
while hearing confessions. The detective
looks down at the blood on the floor and
shakes his head. Then he lifts his eyes
slowly to a huge crucifix. His face softens
as he says to Jesus:

"Who are you? God's son?
No, you know I don't believe that.
I just asked to be polite. . . .
I don't know who you are,
but you are Someone.
Who could miss it? . . .
Do you know how I know?
From what you said. . . . No one on earth
could ever say what you said. . . .
Who could imagine it? . . . Who are you?
What is it that you want from us?"

How would I answer
the detective's last two questions?

I know men, and I tell you
that Jesus Christ is not a man.

NAPOLEON BONAPARTE

"The greatest love
a person can have for his friends
is to give his life for them."

JOHN 15:13

The body of Jesus, nailed to a cross, speaks
a threefold message to those who look
upon it and listen in faith.
First, it is a *sign* of Jesus' love for us,
saying in the most dramatic way possible
what Jesus said so often in his lifetime:
"The greatest love a person can have for
his friends is to give his life for them."
Second, it is an *invitation* to love others
as Jesus loves us, saying what Jesus told
his disciples so often: "Love one another,
just as I love you" (JOHN 15:12).
Third, it is a *revelation,* saying in the
most unmistakable language imaginable
what Jesus told his disciples so often—
love entails suffering: "If anyone wants
to come with me, he must . . . take up his
cross" (LUKE 9:23).

Which of these messages
might God be trying to speak to me—
right now? Why?

God still speaks to those
who take the time to listen.

E. C. McKENZIE

WEEK 29
Day 5 _____

At noon the whole country
was covered with darkness,
which lasted for three hours.
At three o'clock
Jesus cried out with a loud shout,
"Eloi, Eloi, lema sabachthani?"
which means, "My God, my God,
why did you abandon me?"

MARK 15:33-34

There comes a time when we must face
life alone. There comes a time when the
sky turns dark and there's no one but us.
There comes a time when we feel totally
abandoned, even by God. That time came
for Jesus on the cross.

Are there times when I feel
totally abandoned—even by God?
What might these times teach me?

√ *My God, my God,*
why have you abandoned me? . . .
My strength is gone,
gone like water spilled on the ground. . . .
My heart is like melted wax.
My throat is as dry as dust, and my tongue
sticks to the roof of my mouth. . . .
All my bones can be seen.
My enemies look at me and stare.

PSALM 22:1, 14-15, 17

Christ Jesus . . .
gave himself to redeem all mankind.

1 TIMOTHY 2:5-6

In April 1865, the slain body of President
Lincoln lay in state for a few hours in
Cleveland, Ohio. It was on its way from
Washington to Springfield, Illinois, where
it would be buried. In the long line of
people filing past the body was a poor
black woman and her little son. When
they reached the president's body, the
woman lifted up her son and said in a
hushed voice, "Honey, take a long, long
look. That man died for you." What that
mother said about Lincoln, every mother
could say to her child about Jesus. Both
Jesus and Lincoln tell us that waging war
against evil involves great personal
suffering—even the loss of one's own life.

Against what modern evil
would I be willing to wage war and
suffer much—even to losing my life,
if necessary?

It's important
that people know what you stand for.
It's equally important
that they know what you won't *stand for.*

AUTHOR UNKNOWN

WEEK 29
Day 7

[Seeing Jesus die, a Roman officer said,]
"This man was really the Son of God!"

MARK 15:39

The curtain falls on the crucifixion with
all eyes fixed on Jesus. Nothing matters
but that remarkable individual suspended
between heaven and earth. Two thousand
years later, all eyes are still fixed on the
man on the cross. A survivor of the Nazi
holocaust summed up the feeling of millions
when he said:
"As I looked at the man
upon the cross . . . I knew I must
make up my mind once and for all,
and either take a stand beside him and
share in his undefeated faith in God . . .
or else fall . . . into a bottomless pit
of bitterness, hatred, and
unutterable despair."

To what extent
do I come to the same conclusion
that the holocaust survivor did
when I look at the man on the cross?

Love may suffer but it overcomes.
The person of faith has found in Jesus
a hope stronger than history
and a love mightier than death.

ANTHONY PADOVANO (adapted)

WEEKLY MEETING
_____ Sharing Agenda

1 What goes on inside me as I see people spontaneously joining the "Way of the Cross" in Chicago's inner city?

2 When I am in pain, how helpful is it to recall that Jesus suffered and understands what I feel?

3 How might I answer the detective's last two questions about Jesus: Who is Jesus for me? What does Jesus want from me?

4 Which of the three messages of the cross (sign, invitation, revelation) might God be trying to speak to me—right now? Why?

5 Are there times when I feel totally abandoned—even by God? How do I explain such times?

6 Against what modern evil would I be willing to wage war and suffer much—even to losing my life, if necessary?

7 To what extent do I come to the same conclusion that the holocaust survivor did: Either I take a stand beside Jesus and "share in his undefeated faith in God . . . or else fall . . . into a bottomless pit of bitterness, hatred, and unutterable despair"?

IV
VICTORY

The "Fourth Week" of
The Spiritual Exercises of Saint Ignatius
focuses on the mystery of mysteries:
Jesus' resurrection from the dead.

This incredible mystery inspires us
to pray with Saint Paul:

What no one
ever saw or heard,
what no one
ever thought could happen,
is the very thing God prepared
for those who love [God].
1 CORINTHIANS 2:9

30 How well do I understand what happened on Easter?

The Associated Press might have reported the Good Friday events this way:

"JERUSALEM (AP)—Jesus of Nazareth was executed today outside the city walls of this ancient city. Death came at about three o'clock. A sudden thunderstorm scattered the crowd of onlookers and served as a fitting climax to the brief but stormy career of the controversial preacher from the hill country of Galilee. Burial took place immediately. A police guard was posted at the grave site as a precautionary measure. The Galilean is survived by his mother."

Good Friday left Jesus' followers in a state of shock. Their dream that Jesus had come from God to inaugurate God's Kingdom ended in a nightmare.

But in a matter of hours, something incredible took place. Jesus' followers were amazingly transformed. Radiantly alive with new vision and power, they proclaimed the unbelievable message that Jesus had risen.

No amount of persecution could stop them from preaching this "good news." In time, some were crucified themselves. Others were fed to wild beasts in the Roman Colosseum. Still others were burned alive. But the disciples of Jesus could not be silenced.

How can we explain the incredible turn of events that took place on the first Easter? The only acceptable explanation is the one the disciples themselves gave: They had seen Jesus alive!

This week's meditations focus on the mystery of Jesus' resurrection from the dead. The grace you ask for is:

Lord,
release into my heart
the same explosion of joy
that Easter released into your disciples
after they had been plunged
into sadness by Good Friday.

Daily Reading

1	The message	Mt 28:1-7
2	The bribe	Mt 28:11-15
3	The stranger	Lk 24:13-35
4	The gardener	Jn 20:11-18
5	The gift	Jn 20:19-23
6	The doubter	Jn 20:24-29
7	The breakfast	Jn 21:1-7

WEEK 30
Day 1 _____

[Some women arrived at Jesus' tomb.]
Suddenly there was a violent earthquake;
an angel of the Lord came down. . . .
The angel spoke. . . . "I know
you are looking for Jesus. . . .
He has been raised. . . .
Go . . . tell his disciples."

MATTHEW 28:2, 5-7

An old movie concerns archaeologists who
claimed to have found the tomb of Jesus.
To their horror, they also found the
mummified body of Jesus. And so the
gospel's claim that Jesus had been raised
was a lie. The news crushed the Christian
world. Some people were so angered that
they looted churches and burned Bibles.
Years later, one of the archaeologists
confessed on his deathbed that the finding
of the tomb and the body had been
fraudulently choreographed. Whatever the
film's merit, it does help us realize the
great impact Easter had on history.

What is one big way that my life
would be different had Jesus not risen?

The Gospels
do not explain the resurrection;
the resurrection explains the Gospels.

J. S. WHALE

*[When the chief priests and elders
heard about the empty tomb of Jesus,
they bribed the soldiers guarding it,
telling them,] "You are to say that
his disciples came during the night and
stole his body while you were asleep."
The guards . . . did what they were told.*

MATTHEW 28:13, 15

Tomb robbing was not unusual in Jesus'
day. Evidence of this was found in 1878
in Nazareth. It is a marble slab (now in
the Louvre in Paris) containing a Roman
decree stating that anyone who has
"extracted the buried, or has maliciously
transferred them" is to be "sentenced to
capital punishment." Solid scholarship
identifies it as a decree of Claudius
(A.D. 41-54). This puts it in the realm of
possible "secular evidence" witnessing to
the "empty tomb" of Jesus.

What convinces me that Jesus' body was
raised by God, not stolen by the disciples?

*If the disciples had stolen Jesus' body,
is it conceivable that these twelve men
would then have faced death
with radiant courage . . . to propagate
a doctrine which they knew to be false?*

ARNOLD LUNN (slightly adapted)

WEEK 30
Day 3 _____

[The women ran off to tell the apostles.]
The apostles thought that
what the women said was nonsense.

LUKE 24:11

The reaction to the women's story was disbelief. But then Jesus began appearing. For example, on Easter day, two sorrowful disciples were returning to Emmaus. Suddenly a stranger joined them. (It was Jesus, but they didn't recognize him.) When they told him of their sorrow, Jesus explained to them how Scripture had foretold that the Messiah would suffer before entering into his glory. When they reached Emmaus, the disciples invited the stranger to supper. Jesus "took the bread, and said the blessing; then he broke the bread and gave it to them. Then their eyes were opened and they recognized him, but he disappeared. . . . They got up at once and went back to Jerusalem" (LUKE 24:30-31, 33).

When I imagine being one of the disciples, what are my thoughts as Jesus blesses the bread, breaks it, and gives it to me?

[A person] filled with joy
preaches without preaching.

MOTHER TERESA

[The disciples saw Jesus]
but somehow did not recognize him.

LUKE 24:16

A significant feature of Jesus' Easter
appearances is the consistent inability of
his disciples to recognize him. The gospels
cite four different examples of this. These
examples invite us to reflect on an
important fact about resurrection and
Jesus' resurrected body. Resurrection is
not a restoration to life, as with Lazarus
and the widow's son. Resurrection is
something no human person has ever
experienced. It is not a return to a *former*
life, but a quantum leap into a *higher* life.
In other words, the body of Jesus that rose
on Easter was infinitely different from the
body that was buried on Good Friday.

How eagerly do I anticipate sharing
in the risen life Jesus now enjoys? Why?

Why shouldn't you believe
that you will exist again
after this life? . . .
Is it harder for God, . . .
who made your body when it was not,
to make it anew when it has been?

SAINT IRENAEUS

[On Easter night
Jesus appeared to the disciples and
communicated to them a precious gift.
Breathing on them, he said,]
"Receive the Holy Spirit. If you forgive
people's sins, they are forgiven."

JOHN 20:22-23

At first we think, "What an unusual
Easter gift! Why, on Easter night, would
Jesus give his disciples the power to
forgive sins?" After reflecting on it,
however, we realize what a fitting gift it
was. *Forgiveness of sin* sums up the reason
why Jesus died for us. Paul writes, "By
his sacrificial death we are now put right
with God" (ROMANS 5:9). And so Jesus' unusual
Easter gift turns out to be the perfect gift.
The reason? It empowers Jesus' disciples
and their successors to communicate,
personally, to people yet unborn the gift
of forgiveness, which Jesus won for them.

What can I say to Jesus about my need—
and the world's need—
for his Easter gift?

*The penalty of sin is to face,
not the anger of Jesus,
but the heartbreak in his eyes.*

WILLIAM BARCLAY

*[Thomas was absent on Easter night
when Jesus appeared to the apostles.
So he doubted, saying he'd believe only
when he put his finger in Jesus' wounds.
A week later, Jesus reappeared.
This time, Thomas was present.
Jesus showed Thomas his wounds, saying,]*
"Stop your doubting and believe!"
Thomas answered him,
"My Lord and my God!" *Jesus said to him,*
"Do you believe because you see me?
How happy are those who believe
without seeing me!"

JOHN 20:27-29

Calvin Miller's book *The Song* contains a
story about a woman who had no faith in
God. She married and had three sons.
Then tragedy struck. One by one the three
sons died. At the funeral of the first son,
she was a *nonbeliever*. At the funeral of
the second, she became a *seeker*. At the
funeral of the third son, she wept and
became a *believer*.

What are some memorable moments
along my own journey to faith in Jesus?

*The question is never "Faith or no faith?"
It's always "In whom do I put my faith?"*

ANONYMOUS

WEEK 30
Day 7 _____

[Jesus said,]
"Simon son of John, do you love me?"

JOHN 21:16

A delightful resurrection appearance took place when Peter and the others were rowing to shore after a bad night of fishing. A stranger appeared on the beach and told them to recast their net. They did, and it was filled with fish. John looked again at the stranger and gasped, "It is the Lord!" When the disciples reached the beach, they saw Jesus had prepared breakfast. They all ate. Then Jesus did something unusual. He turned to Peter and asked him three times, "Do you love me?" Three times Peter answered, "Yes, Lord!" And three times Jesus responded to Peter, "Take care of my sheep." Peter's triple affirmation of love erased from his heart his triple denial of Jesus. And Jesus' threefold response to Peter commissioned him to be the shepherd of Jesus' followers (JOHN 21).

Imagining I'm Peter, what are my thoughts that night as I lie awake unable to sleep?

Is it any wonder that to this day this Galilean is too much for our small hearts?
H. G. WELLS

WEEKLY MEETING
Sharing Agenda

1 What is one big way that my life would be different right now had Jesus not risen?

2 What convinces me that Jesus' body was raised by God, not stolen by the disciples?

3 When I imagined being one of the disciples eating supper with Jesus at Emmaus, what were some thoughts I had as I watched Jesus bless the bread, break it, and give it to me?

4 How eagerly do I anticipate sharing in the risen life that Jesus now enjoys? Why?

5 What need does our world have, in a special way today, for Jesus' Easter gift? How well am I making use of this great gift?

6 What are some memorable moments along my own journey to faith in Jesus?

7 When I imagined I was Peter, what thoughts went through my mind as I lay awake unable to sleep after Jesus asked me three times "Do you love me?"

31 How does Easter impact my everyday life?

The famous Hollywood film director Cecil B. DeMille was reading a book while drifting in a canoe on a lake in northern Maine. He happened to look away from the book, momentarily, down into the water. There he saw a swarm of beetles playing on the surface.

Suddenly one of the beetles crawled halfway up the side of the canoe, stuck the talons of its legs into the wood, and died. DeMille returned to his book.

About three hours later DeMille happened to look down at the dead beetle again. What he saw amazed him. The beetle had dried up, and its back had split open. As he watched, something began to emerge from the split: first a head, then wings, then a tail. It was a beautiful dragonfly. After it flew away, DeMille took his finger and nudged the dried-out shell of the beetle. It was like a tomb.

What happened to the beetle helps to give us an insight into what happened to Jesus.

Jesus died nailed to the cross—as the beetle died fastened to the canoe. Jesus

underwent an amazing transformation
three days after he died—as the beetle
underwent a similar transformation three
hours after it died. Finally, the transformed
body of Jesus had new powers to move
about—as the transformed body of the
beetle could now fly and no longer had
to crawl.

This week's meditations focus on the
central mystery of Christianity: that the
risen Jesus is alive and active in our world.
The grace you ask for is:

Loving Father,
fill my heart with the joy
that flows from the knowledge
that your risen Son's loving presence
permeates our world;
and help me open
my mind, my heart, and my soul to it.

Daily Reading

1 Like fire burning   Lk 24:28–35
2 To him be glory   Eph 3:14–21
3 Death to life   Rom 6:3–11
4 Hidden in Christ   Col 3:1–17
5 Filled with awe   Acts 2:43–47
6 Today and forever   Heb 13:1–8
7 A chosen people   1 Pt 2:1–10

WEEK 31
Day 1 _____

*You have rescued me from death
and kept me from defeat.
And so I walk in the presence of God.*

PSALM 56:13

A small boy and his grandfather were
flying a kite on a high hill. The kite soared
into the sky. Then suddenly a low cloud
hid it from sight. After a few minutes the
grandfather said, "Robbie, maybe some
thief in that cloud stole your kite!" Robbie
shook his head. "But, Robbie, how can you
be sure that kite's still at the end of your
string?" The boy said, "Because I can feel
what you can't. I can feel the kite tug at
my string." That story illustrates why
many people who weren't blessed to see
Jesus after his resurrection were sure,
nonetheless, he had risen. They could feel
the "tug" of the risen Jesus in their lives.
They could feel the power of the risen
Jesus at work in their hearts.

What is one way I feel the "tug"
of the Christ in my life right now?

*As all people die because of their union
with Adam, . . .
all will be raised to life
because of their union with Christ.*

1 CORINTHIANS 15:22

*His power working in us is able to do
so much more than we can ever ask for,
or even think of.*

EPHESIANS 3:20

A deeply disturbed college girl was flying
home to Rhode Island for the Easter
holidays. Her school year was nearly over,
and it had been a disaster. Once home, she
drove to the ocean. She writes:
"I just sat there in the moonlight
watching the waves roll up on the beach.
Slowly my disastrous first year passed
before my eyes. . . . Then all of a sudden
the whole experience fell into place. . . .
The next thing I knew, the sun was
coming up. . . . All my old goals and
enthusiasm came rushing back stronger
than ever. I rose with the sun,
got into my car, and drove home."
After her Easter vacation, the girl returned
to college, picked up the pieces, and
finished the year successfully. In the short
span of an Easter vacation she had died
and risen to a new life.

Can I recall a similar resurrection
experience in my own life?

The dream is yours, claim it.
WALTER FAUNTROY

*[In baptism] we were buried with him
and shared his death, in order that,
just as Christ was raised from death
by the glorious power of the Father,
so also we might live a new life.*

ROMANS 6:4

Darryl Stingley was a wide receiver for
the New England Patriots in the 1970s.
He was injured in a game against the
Oakland Raiders and left paralyzed from
the chest down. Today he can use only
one hand and moves about in an electric
wheelchair. Darryl insists that in some
ways his life is better now than formerly.
Recalling his playing days, he says, "I had
tunnel vision. All I wanted was to be the
best athlete I could, and a lot of other
things were overlooked. Now I've come
back to them. This is a rebirth for me."
That statement by Darryl testifies to the
power of the resurrection at work in
people's lives today—a power so strong
that it can bring forth life from death.

How did an apparent personal tragedy
result in a spiritual rebirth for me?

*Immortal Hope dispels the gloom!
An angel sits beside the tomb.*

SARAH FLOWER ADAMS

*You have been raised to life with Christ,
so set your hearts on the things
that are in heaven.*

COLOSSIANS 3:1

In 1963 Brian Sternberg was the world's
pole vault champ. One night he came
down on the edge of a trampoline and was
totally paralyzed. He became bitter. But
faith worked a remarkable transformation
in him. Five years later Brian was carried
onto a stage. His skinny arms and legs
dangled like those of a rag doll over the
arms of Wes Wilmer, a big football player.
Propping Brian up in a chair, Wes put a
mike to his mouth. In a soft voice, Brian
spoke to a convention of athletes:
"My friends . . . I pray to God
that what has happened to me
will never happen to one of you. . . .
I pray to God you will never know
the pain that I live with daily. . . .
Unless, my friends, that's what it takes
for you to put God in the center
of your life."

What might Jesus be saying to me
through Brian's amazing statement?

"I am the resurrection and the life."

JOHN 11:25

WEEK 31
Day 5 _____

*With great power the apostles gave witness
to the resurrection of the Lord.*

ACTS 4:33

A young man wrote:
"I'm a very logical, scientific-minded
person. I need proofs for everything.
Yet, something has happened to me here
in college that I can't explain rationally,
scientifically, or even psychologically.
I've become totally preoccupied
with Jesus Christ, who I somehow feel
is working within me. . . .
I can't explain this feeling. It came about
mainly these past few months, when I
began reading about the early Christians.
I was so amazed and in awe of these people
that I found it impossible to question Jesus
or doubt who he is—the Son of God. . . .
Call it crazy, psychotic, or whatever. . . .
I can't explain it, nor does it go away."
ROBERT RYBICKI (slightly adapted)

Do I make an effort to nourish my faith
by daily or regular spiritual reading?

*God is not an idea, or a definition
that we have committed to memory;
[God] is a presence
that we experience in our hearts.*

LOUIS EVELY

Jesus Christ is the same
yesterday, today, and forever.

HEBREWS 13:8

"Let us rejoice. . . .
No one is shut out from this joy. . . .
Let the saint rejoice
as he sees the palm of victory at hand.
Let the sinner rejoice
as he sees the hand of forgiveness. . . .
Christian, remember your dignity. . . .
Do not forget
that you have been rescued
from the power of darkness and
brought into the light of God's kingdom."

SAINT LEO THE GREAT

What is there about Jesus' resurrection
that makes me rejoice,
especially at this moment in my life?

All we want in Christ,
we find in Christ.
If we want little,
we shall find little.
If we want much, we shall find much;
but if, in utter helplessness,
we cast our all on Christ,
he will be to us
the whole treasury of God.

HENRY BENJAMIN WHIPPLE

WEEK 31
Day 7

[Jesus said,]
"I will be with you always,
to the end of the age."
MATTHEW 28:20

The resurrection of Jesus invites us to
open our hearts to the presence of the
risen Jesus in today's world. It invites us
to let Jesus do for us what he has done for
so many. It invites us to love again, after
our love has been rejected and we are
tempted to hate. It invites us to hope
again, after our hope has been dashed to
pieces and we are tempted to despair.
It invites us to believe again, after our
belief has been shaken and we are tempted
to doubt. It invites us to pick up the
broken pieces and start again, after
discouragement has crushed us and we
want to quit. The resurrection is the good
news that Jesus is alive and active in our
world, ready to work miracles in our lives,
if we but let him.

Which of the above invitations
do I feel that Jesus
might be holding out to me right now?

We are Easter People;
and Alleluia is our song.
SAINT AUGUSTINE

WEEKLY MEETING
Sharing Agenda

1 What is one way I feel the "tug" of the Christ in my life right now?

2 Can I recall a resurrection experience in my life similar to the one the college girl experienced on her Easter vacation?

3 Did an apparent personal tragedy ever turn out to be a rebirth for me?

4 What might Jesus be saying to me through Brian Sternberg's amazing statement?

5 Do I try to deepen and nourish my faith by some kind of regular spiritual reading?

6 What do I personally find in Jesus' resurrection that makes me rejoice, especially at this time in my life?

7 Which of the invitations described in Day 7 do I feel the resurrection of Jesus might be holding out to me right now?

32 How joyfully do I continue the work Jesus began?

Canadian student Terry Fox lost his leg to bone cancer. He had only a few years to live, and he wanted to use the time as significantly as possible.

Terry decided to run across Canada, invite people to sponsor him, and give the money to cancer research. For eighteen months he trained on his artificial leg. On April 12, 1980, he dipped his limb into the Atlantic Ocean and began his run. In his pocket were pledges totaling $1 million.

Four months and three thousand miles into the run, Terry collapsed. The cancer had spread to his lungs. When news about Terry flashed across Canada, money poured into the hospital. Before Terry died a short time later, the total reached $24 million.

There's a sequel to that incredibly courageous story. Donald Marrs of Cincinnati was a cancer victim like Terry. He was so moved by Terry's spirit that he decided to finish his run.

Donald began below Chicago. Three months later he reached the Golden Gate Bridge. A drizzle was falling as he crossed it. And when he dipped his hand into the

Pacific Ocean, a rainbow arced across the sky.

This inspiring sequel contains an important message. Terry is like Jesus, who began a noble work on earth but died before he could finish it. We are like Donald Marrs. We are being invited to take the baton from Jesus' hand and finish the work he began. This is what the feast of the Ascension is all about: the passing of the baton from Jesus to his followers.

This week's meditations focus on the ascension and its invitation. The grace you ask for is:

Lord, may the spirit and power
of your risen presence
fill my heart with a desire
to complete the noble work you began.

Daily Reading

1	Be my witnesses	Acts 1:1-9
2	I'll be with you	Mt 28:16-20
3	Really the Savior	Jn 4:34-42
4	Remain in me	Jn 15:1-9
5	Don't stand there	Acts 1:9-11
6	Don't be afraid	Is 35:1-4
7	I make all things new	Rev 21:1-7

WEEK 32
Day 1

*[Before ascending to heaven,
Jesus said to his disciples,]*
*"When the Holy Spirit comes upon you . . .
you will be witnesses for me in Jerusalem,
in all of Judea and Samaria,
and to the ends of the earth."*

ACTS 1:8

The high point in a relay race is the
moment when one runner passes the
baton to another runner. More races are
won or lost at that moment than at any
other moment in the race. The passing of
the baton in a relay race is a good image
of the ascension. Jesus passes the baton
to his disciples. He passes on to us the
responsibility to make God's Kingdom a
living reality in our homes, our schools,
and our world.

How is the work I am doing right now
helping to make God's Kingdom
a living reality on earth?
What might I do to make my work
even more of a help than it is?

*Now I get me up to work,
I pray the Lord I may not shirk,
And if I die before tonight,
I pray my work will be all right.*
THOMAS OSBORNE DAVIS

[Jesus said to his disciples,]
"Proclaim the gospel to every creature."

MARK 16:15 (NAB)

Composer Giacomo Puccini was stricken
by cancer while working on his last opera,
Turandot. He said to his students, "If I
don't finish it, finish it for me." Shortly
afterward, he died. His students carried
out his wish. In 1926 Puccini's favorite
student, Arturo Toscanini, directed the
premiere in Milan. When the opera reached
the point where Puccini was forced to put
down his pen, Toscanini stopped the
music, turned to the audience, and cried
out, "Thus far the Master wrote, but he
died." A reverent silence filled the opera
house. Then Toscanini picked up the
baton again, smiled through his tears, and
cried out, "But the disciples finished his
work." At the conclusion of the opera,
the audience broke into a tumultuous
applause.

How prepared and willing am I
to help finish my Master's work?

*[The ascension] does not represent
Jesus' removal from the earth, but his
constant presence everywhere on earth.*

WILLIAM TEMPLE

WEEK 32
Day 3 _____

*[Jesus said,] "The harvest is large,
but there are few workers."*
MATTHEW 9:37

Kate Drexel came from a wealthy family
in Philadelphia. Riding through the city
one day in the 1880s, Kate saw the tragic
plight of African-American children living
in hideous slum conditions. When she
probed their plight, she became convinced
that prejudice, broken promises, and unjust
laws were creating a cycle of ignorance
and powerlessness for these children.
Kate decided to do something. She founded
the Sisters of the Blessed Sacrament to
work among African-American and Native
American children. By the time Mother
Katherine Drexel died, she had spent
nearly $20 million of her own personal
fortune on this work. The order she
founded a hundred years ago continues
her work.

If I had $20 million to spend as I wished,
what is one thing I would use it for
immediately? Why this?

*Practical people
would be a lot more practical
if they were just a little more dreamy.*
J. P. McEVOY

[Jesus said to his disciples,]
"I chose you and appointed you
to go and bear . . . fruit that endures."

JOHN 15:16

A traveler came upon a barren hillside in
the French Alps. In the middle of it he saw
an old man with a sack of acorns on his
back and an iron pipe in his hand. The
man was punching holes in the ground
with the pipe and planting the acorns in
the holes. Later the old man told the
traveler that his wife and son had died,
and this was how he spent his days. "I
want to do something useful," he said.
Twenty-five years later the traveler
returned to the same hillside. It was
covered with a forest two miles wide and
five miles long. Birds were singing, animals
were playing, and wildflowers were
blooming. The traveler was amazed at
how beautiful the hillside was.

What trees am I planting?
What trees might I plant?

The person who plants few seeds
will have a small crop;
the one who plants many seeds
will have a large crop.

2 CORINTHIANS 9:6

[After Jesus ascended to heaven,]
two men dressed in white
suddenly stood beside [the apostles]
and said, . . . "This Jesus . . .
will come back in the same way
that you saw him go to heaven."

ACTS 1:10-11

A mother was lying on a crowded beach.
Suddenly her five-year-old son, Chase,
began shouting, "Jesus is coming!" The
mother looked up. Chase was pointing
excitedly to a plane towing a banner
reading "Jesus is coming." After the plane
passed, Chase asked, "So when's he
coming, Mom?" His mother did a quick
search of her mind. Then she said, "The
Bible says at a time when we least
expect." Chase paused for a long time.
Then, looking around at the people sunning
themselves on the beach, he said with a
certain amount of concern in his voice,
"Do you think everybody's ready, Mom?"

If I were Chase's mother,
how would I answer his question?

Of all sad words of tongue and pen,
The saddest are these:
"It might have been."

JOHN GREENLEAF WHITTIER

Tell everyone who is discouraged,
"Be strong and don't be afraid!
God is coming to your rescue."

ISAIAH 35:4

In *God of the Oppressed,* James Cone asks
concerning pre-Civil War days:
"How could black slaves know
that they were somebody
when everything in their environment
said they were nobody?" He responds:
"Only because they knew
that Christ was present with them
and that his presence included
the divine promise to come again
and take them to the 'New Jerusalem.' "
A similar promise sustained faithful Jews
in ancient times. It was the divine promise
that God, in the person of the Messiah,
was coming to their rescue.

What sustains me
in my moments of fear, depression,
or discouragement?

I have learned this secret,
so that anywhere, at any time, . . .
I have the strength
to face all conditions
by the power that Christ gives me.

PHILIPPIANS 4:12-13

WEEK 32
Day 7 _____

*Christ . . . will appear a second time,
not to deal with sin, but to save those
who are waiting for him.*

HEBREWS 9:28

A Negro spiritual expresses the longing
of early American black slaves for the
Second Coming of Jesus:
"There's a king and captain high,
And he's coming by and by,
And he'll find me hoeing cotton
when he comes.
You can hear his legions charging
in the regions of the sky,
And he'll find me hoeing cotton
when he comes. . . .
He'll be crowned by saints and angels
when he comes,
They'll be shouting out Hosanna!
to the man that men denied,
And I'll kneel among my cotton
when he comes."

This spiritual prompts a question:
If Jesus' Second Coming—or my death—
were to come tomorrow, what is one way
it would change my plans today?

*The past is yours, learn from it.
The present is yours, fulfill it.*

WALTER FAUNTROY

WEEKLY MEETING
Sharing Agenda

1 How is the work I am doing right now helping to make God's Kingdom a living reality on earth? What might I do to make my work even more of a help than it is?

2 How prepared and willing am I to help complete the Master's work?

3 If I had $20 million to spend as I wished, what is one thing I would use it for immediately? Why this?

4 What trees am I planting that will make the world a better place because I lived? What trees might I consider planting?

5 If I were Chase's mother, how would I answer his question about whether the people lying on the beach sunning themselves were ready for Jesus' Second Coming?

6 What sustains me in my moments of discouragement, depression, or fear?

7 If Jesus' Second Coming—or my death—were to come tomorrow, what is one way it would change my plans today?

33 How clearly do I see Jesus in his Church?

During the cold-war years, Communist officials built a giant television tower in East Berlin. Just below its tip, they constructed a revolving restaurant.

The Communists intended the structure to be a showpiece to the West. But a fluke in design turned it into an embarrassment to its atheistic builders. Whenever the sun hit the tower and the restaurant at a certain angle, it turned them into a blazing cross. Officials repainted the tower to destroy the dramatic phenomena, but to no avail.

Something similar happened in Jerusalem after Jesus' crucifixion. Officials hoped Jesus' death on the cross would destroy the Christian movement. But just the opposite happened. The movement spread spectacularly.

What caused the tiny mustard seed of Christianity to mushroom into a great tree in such a short time? Exactly what Jesus said would happen. The Holy Spirit came upon the disciples on Pentecost. And neither the disciples nor the world were ever the same again.

This week's meditations focus on the coming of the Holy Spirit on the followers of Jesus. The grace you ask for is:

*Lord, help me see your Church
as it really is: an extension of
your risen body into space and time.
And may the darkness
of its human dimension (members)
never obscure the brightness
of its divine dimension (head).*

Daily Reading

WEEK 33
Day 1 _____

There was a noise from the sky
which sounded like a strong wind. . . .
Then they saw what looked like
tongues of fire which spread out
and touched each person there.

ACTS 2:2-3

Jews saw a link between the wind and
God. The wind's breathlike touch and
stormlike force spoke of God's gentle
presence and mighty power. The prophets
used the wind as an image of God's Spirit
(EZEKIEL 37:9-10). Jesus did too (JOHN 3:8). Jews saw
an even greater link between fire and
God. This grew out of Moses' experience
of God in the burning bush and the
people's experience of God on the burning
mountain (EXODUS 19:16-18). It is against this
background that we must read about the
Holy Spirit's coming.

Why is fire, especially,
a fitting symbol of the Holy Spirit?
Can I imagine the Holy Spirit
coming upon me right now
as sounding wind and searing fire?

Holy Spirit, fill my heart
with the flame of your love.
Flood my mind
with the light of your truth.

There were Jews living in Jerusalem . . .
from every country in the world.
When they heard this noise [wind],
a large crowd gathered.

ACTS 2:5-6

Excitedly, Peter went out and explained
to the crowd what had happened.
"When the people heard this,
they were deeply troubled
and said to Peter and the other apostles,
'What shall we do, brothers?'
Peter said to them, 'Each one of you
must turn away from his sins and
be baptized in the name of Jesus Christ,
so that your sins will be forgiven;
and you will receive God's gift,
the Holy Spirit' " (ACTS 2:37-38).

How helpful is it to read the prayer below
slowly, audibly, and with deep yearning?

Breathe on me, Spirit of God,
that I may think what is holy.
Drive me, Spirit of God,
that I may do what is holy.
Strengthen me, Spirit of God,
that I may preserve what is holy.
Guide me, Spirit of God,
that I may never lose what is holy.

SAINT AUGUSTINE (adapted)

[Jesus] is the head of his body,
the church;
he is the source of the body's life.

COLOSSIANS 1:18

Before his conversion, Saint Paul was on
a journey to arrest some Christians.
Suddenly a light flashed round about him.
"He fell to the ground
and heard a voice saying to him,
'Saul, Saul! Why do you persecute me?'
'Who are you, Lord?' he asked.
'I am Jesus, whom you persecute,'
the voice said" (ACTS 9:4-5).
Paul was baffled. He wasn't persecuting
Jesus—only his followers. Then it hit
him. Jesus and his followers formed one
body. Paul wrote later, "We are one body
in union with Christ" (ROMANS 12:5).

How much do I find my mind in accord
with the statement below? Why?

Someone said to a young woman,
"I can find Christ in my own way.
I don't need the Church."
The young woman said to the person,
"You stand a better chance of finding
your head apart from your body than
of finding the risen Christ apart from
his Church. They can't be separated."

[Jesus said,] "You are like light
for the whole world. . . .
Your light must shine before people."
MATTHEW 5:14, 16

A teacher asked her students, "What if
an incredible explosion destroyed all life
on earth except for the thirty of us in this
room? Where would the Church be?" They
thought a minute. Then a boy said, "It
would be in this room. We would be the
Church." That story makes an important
point. The Church is not a *place* where
people gather. It is the *people* who gather.
To have Church we must gather. It's like
the bread that we use for the Eucharist.
Hundreds of grains of wheat must be
gathered to make it. In a similar way,
only by gathering do we make the risen
Christ visible in today's world. Jesus
assured us, "Where two or three come
together in my name, I am there with
them" (MATTHEW 18:20).

What tends to keep me from gathering
on the Lord's Day at the Lord's table?

If you find a perfect church,
by all means join it!
Then it will no longer be perfect.
BILLY GRAHAM

WEEK 33
Day 5 _____

The church is Christ's body.
EPHESIANS 1:23

A college girl said to her new roommate, "I respect your belief, but I find it hard to believe the Church is Christ's Body when I see the way some Christians act." The girl said, "I felt the same way until I remembered that I don't find it hard to believe Beethoven is a genius when I hear the way some musicians play his music. Beethoven isn't the problem; the musicians are. So, too, the Church isn't the problem; its members are."

To what extent am I a "problem"?

I think I shall never see
a Church that's all it ought to be:
A Church whose members never stray
beyond the straight and narrow way.
A Church that has no empty pews,
whose pastor never has the blues.

A church whose deacon's always "Deak"
and none are proud and all are meek.
Such perfect Churches there may be,
but none of them are known to me.
But still, we'll work and pray and plan
to make our own the best we can.

AUTHOR UNKNOWN

We are one body in . . . Christ. . . .
So we are to use our different gifts
in accordance with the grace
that God has given us.

ROMANS 12:5-6

A senior citizens' complex in Buffalo,
Minnesota, combines a retirement home
with a day-care center. The administrator
says, "As hard as we try to keep our
residents active and alert, those kids do a
better job just doing what kids do. Their
life, youth, and energy keep everybody
stimulated." And the children are also
winners. They have no problem looking
beyond wrinkles and gray hair to the
heart. What they're looking for is "a hug,
a lap, a kind word, a touch, somebody to
read them a story, somebody to smile and
share with."

How effectively am I using the gifts
that God has given me
to enrich the Body of Christ?
What is one way
I might begin imitating the children
and look "beyond wrinkles and gray hair
to the heart"?

The rising tide lifts all the boats.

JOHN F. KENNEDY

WEEK 33
Day 7 _____

*[You] are built upon the foundation
laid by the apostles and prophets,
the cornerstone being Christ. . . .
[He] holds the whole building together
and makes it grow into a sacred temple.*

EPHESIANS 2:20-21

Years ago a TV show featured an artist
who invited kids to make a few scribbles
on a clean sheet of paper. Then the artist
would create something beautiful out of
the scribbles. One scribble became a girl's
ponytail; another became a boy's arm. In
a sense, that's what God wants from us.
God wants to take our weaknesses—our
scribbles—and create something beautiful
out of them. God wants to do even more.
God wants to unite us to Jesus, empower
us with the Holy Spirit, and fashion us
into the living temple of the divine
presence in our world.

How ready am I
to give God whatever I have,
believing that God will, indeed,
create something beautiful out of it?

*You must shine . . .
like stars lighting up the sky.*

PHILIPPIANS 2:15

1 How helpful did I find imagining the Holy Spirit coming upon me as sounding wind and searing fire?

2 How helpful did I find reading the prayer to the Holy Spirit slowly, audibly, and with desire?

3 If the Church is Christ's Body, what ought to be my attitude toward it? In point of fact, what is my attitude toward it?

4 What tends to keep me from gathering on the Lord's Day at the Lord's table?

5 To what extent am I a "problem"? In other words, do I make it easier or harder for other people to believe that the Church is the Body of Christ? How?

6 What are some special gifts I have? How effectively am I using them to enrich the Body of Christ?

7 How ready am I to take the baton from the hand of Jesus and strive to make his Church into what he intended it to be: a star shining in the night sky of our world?

34 How clearly do I see God in all things?

(Contemplation: God's Presence)

Some years ago the *Chicago Tribune* carried an article entitled "Taking a Walk with My Grandson," by Amelia Dahl. It was written in dialogue form and went something like this:

Ricky: Grandma, why do trees take off their clothes in the fall?

Grandma: Because they're worn out and must be turned in for new ones.

Ricky: Where do they get new ones?

Grandma: From the ground, where Mother Nature is busy preparing a new spring wardrobe for them.

Ricky: Ever notice how the sky looks like an upside-down lake?

Grandma: And the little white clouds look like sailboats, don't they?

Ricky: I wonder where they're sailing to.

Grandma: Maybe to a cloud meeting.

Ricky: What would they do there?

Grandma: Probably decide if the earth needs more rain.

Ricky: Gee, God thinks of everything, doesn't he, Grandma?

Ricky's grandma is a beautiful example of someone who has kept a childlike wonder.

To wonder means to see things as a child does: with the newness they had when they tumbled from the creative hand of God. It means to be able to see in the eyes of a friend the love of God.

This week's meditations focus on the wonder-filled world that God created. The grace you ask for is:

Lord, help me see the world
with the same beauty it had
when it tumbled from your creative hand.
Help me see that
"nothing here below is profane.
On the contrary, everything is sacred."

TEILHARD DE CHARDIN

Weekly Instruction

During the week you may wish to go for an occasional "prayer walk" by yourself. If you can do this at sunrise or sunset by a lake or in a park, great!

Daily Reading

1	The LORD created all	Ps 104:19-24
2	The LORD protects all	Ps 40:1-5
3	The LORD is king of all	Ps 93
4	The LORD is in all	Acts 17:22-28
5	Make music to the LORD	Ps 150
6	Praise the LORD	Ps 104:1-15
7	The LORD is great	Ps 145

WEEK 34
Day 1 ─────────────────────

[The LORD] has decided the number
of the stars and calls each one by name.
Great and mighty is our Lord.

PSALM 147:4-5

World-famous musician Pablo Casals said,
"I *find* God in the smallest
and in the largest things.
I *see* God in colors and designs. . . .
Think of how no two grains of sand
are alike; how there is not one nose,
one voice like another; how, among
billions and billions of living and
nonliving things in the Universe
no two are exactly alike.
Who but God could do that?"

To what extent am I like Casals
in being able to find the Creator
in creation: in things like a sandy beach,
a flower bed, the faces of friends?
Why are some people, like artists,
able to do this better than others?

God is the Dancer, . . .
Creation is the Dance. . . .
Be silent and look at the Dance . . .
a star, a flower, a fading leaf. . . .
And hopefully it won't be long
before you see . . . the Dancer.

ANTHONY DE MELLO

_The light of the sun shines down
on everything, and everything is filled
with the Lord's glory._

SIRACH 42:16

A man stood on the edge of a cliff in Italy
with suicide on his mind. Suddenly he
heard music so pure that it startled him.
He looked around. What he saw amazed
him. There at the entrance to a cave stood
a barefoot boy playing a harmonica. The
sound of the music and the sight of the
boy touched the depths of his tortured
soul. Suddenly the man realized how
much loveliness and beauty were in the
world. He said later that the barefoot boy
playing the harmonica was a gift from
God. It was much more. It was the
presence and the power of God entering
his life to help him at a time when he could
not help himself.

Can I recall when the sight or the sound
of something beautiful touched me and
raised my mind and heart to God?

_God sent his Singers upon earth
With songs of sadness and of mirth,
That they might touch the hearts of men,
And bring them back to heaven again._

HENRY WADSWORTH LONGFELLOW

WEEK 34
Day 3 _____

"Be still, and know that I am God!"
PSALM 46:10

One drizzly morning Barry Lopez got up
early and went for a walk in the woods.
As he trailed along under the pines and
the cedars, he recalled seeing his
grandfather go off through these same
woods years before. When Barry reached
a clearing, he knelt down on the damp
earth. It gave him a feeling of being united
with God and God's creation. Half an hour
later Barry headed back to the house. He
felt renewed. Then he remembered why
his grandfather used to go for morning
walks in the woods. It was his way of
saying his morning prayers. He would
always end up on the other side of the
woods, standing on the beach, with his
hands in his pockets, gazing at the ocean.

How cheated do I feel that I have no woods
or ocean to help me pray in the morning?
What would I say to someone
who felt very cheated because of this?

Think often on God,
by day, by night, in your business,
and even in your diversions.
God is always near you and with you.
BROTHER LAWRENCE

*[Paul said,] "God is
actually not far from any one of us; . . .
'In him we live and move and exist.' "*

ACTS 17:27-28

Herman Melville was one of eight children.
His family lived in poverty in New York
City. His schooling stopped when he was
fifteen. At twenty, he took a job as a cabin
boy on a ship that sailed to England. Thus
began a great romance with the sea.
Eventually, Herman wrote the famous sea
novel *Moby Dick.* A passage in it reads:
"If the great sun moves not of himself;
but as an errand boy in heaven;
nor one single star can revolve,
but by some invisible power;
how can this one small heart beat;
this one small brain think thoughts;
unless God does that beating,
does that thinking."

How easily do I find God in the world?
What is one stumbling block
that keeps me from finding God?

*I sought to hear the voice of God,
And climbed the topmost steeple.
But God declared: "Go down again—
I dwell among the people."*

LOUIS NEWMAN

WEEK 34
Day 5 _____

"The LORD . . . is in this place."
GENESIS 28:16

A high school student wrote:
"I got up Sunday morning depressed.
I don't know why, because this was the day
of the big rock concert at Hawthorne.
Waiting in line at the racetrack, however,
my depression began to fade. Once inside,
we sprawled on the grass with thousands
of others—70,000. There was a great sound
system, so the music really energized me.
When the second band finished, I looked
around me. Wow! What a great sight!
I was really starting to feel good, now.
Then the last band opened with a rock
classic. Everyone as far as I could see
was standing up, clapping their hands, and
moving to the music. A fantastic feeling
rushed over me. Then I thought, amid these
super-great sounds, God must be present.
God has to be!" (slightly adapted)

Can I recall a time when I felt
God's presence, as the student did?

When I am operating,
I feel the presence of God so real
that I cannot tell
where [God's] skill ends and mine begins.
ANONYMOUS SURGEON

O Lord, our Lord,
your greatness is seen in all the world!

PSALM 8:1

A father took his young son on a camping
trip in the Adirondack Mountains in New
York. To make the trip more enjoyable,
he hired an experienced guide to accompany
them. The guide led them off the beaten
trails and took them into the heart of the
great forest. The boy was amazed at how
the old guide spotted things that the
ordinary person missed. One day, after
the guide had been pointing out some
hidden beauties in the forest, the boy
exclaimed, "I'll bet you can even see God
out here!" The old guide replied, "Son, it's
getting hard for me to see anything else
but God out here."

Can I recall the last time I paused
to listen to a songbird?
To marvel at a sunset?
What keeps me from doing these things?

Earth's crammed with heaven,
And every common bush afire with God.
But only he who sees takes off his shoes;
The rest sit round it
and pluck blackberries.

E. B. BROWNING

WEEK 34
Day 7 _____

O Lord, my God, how great you are!

PSALM 104:1

"I sing the mighty power of God,
That made the mountains rise;
That spread the flowing seas abroad,
And built the lofty skies. . . .

"I sing the goodness of the Lord,
That filled the earth with food;
He formed the creatures with his word,
And then pronounced them good.
Lord, how your wonders are displayed,
Where e'er I turn my eye:
If I survey the ground I tread,
Or gaze upon the sky!

"There's not a plant or flower below,
But makes your glories known;
And clouds arise and tempests blow,
By order from your throne;
While all that borrows life from you
Is ever in your care,
And everywhere that man can be,
You, God, are present there."

ISAAC WATTS (1713)

As I reread this hymn meditatively,
what phrase strikes me most? Why?

If God seems far away, guess who moved!

AUTHOR UNKNOWN

WEEKLY MEETING
Sharing Agenda

1 What part of God's creation speaks to me most about the Creator, and what does it say to me?

2 Can I recall when the sight or the sound of something beautiful raised my mind and heart to God?

3 Can I recall a walk along a trail or a beach that lifted my thoughts to God and renewed my spirit?

4 How easily do I find God, and what is one stumbling block that keeps me from finding God more easily?

5 Can I recall a game, a concert, or a time with friends when I sensed God's presence?

6 When was the last time I paused to marvel at something in nature? Why don't I do it more often?

7 What phrase in Isaac Watts's hymn struck me most? Why?

35 How clearly do I see God's love in all things?
(Contemplation: God's Love)

The life of astronaut Jim Irwin was changed forever after his voyage to the moon aboard *Apollo 15*. Irwin writes in his book *To Rule the Night*:

"I wish I had been a writer or a poet,
so that I could convey adequately
the feeling of this flight. . . .
It has been
sort of a slow-breaking revelation for me.
The ultimate effect has been
to deepen and strengthen
all the religious insight I ever had.
It has remade my faith. . . .
On the moon the total picture
of the power of God
and his Son Jesus Christ
became abundantly clear to me."

What happened to Jim Irwin must happen to each of us. We must also discover God not as someone remote from us, but as someone closer to us than our own breath. We must experience God as someone who loves us more deeply than we love ourselves.

This week's meditations seek to bring you face-to-face with the mystery of God's love—for you. The grace you ask before each meditation is:

Lord, help me discover and experience the mystery of your loving presence in every dimension of my life.

Daily Reading

1	I long for God	Ps 63:1-8
2	I belong to God	Ps 95:1-7
3	God's love saved me	Ps 116:1-14
4	Give thanks to God	Ps 107:23-32
5	God is love	1 Jn 4:7-12
6	God's love is eternal	Ps 136:1-9
7	God's love engulfs us	Rom 8:35-39

WEEK 35
Day 1

O LORD, my God, how great you are! . . .
You use the clouds as your chariot
and ride on the wings of the wind. . . .
Praise the LORD, my soul!

Psalm 104:1, 3, 35

The film *Lili* portrays a young girl in a
traveling circus. Since there are few girls
her age in the circus, her closest friends
are three puppets in one of the sideshows.
As Lili grows older, she grows lonelier.
One day she gets so lonely she decides to
run away. As she hugs the puppets
good-bye, she feels them trembling.
Suddenly she realizes that it's not the
puppets who love her, but the young
puppeteer. The puppets are merely the
means he uses to express his love.

To what extent am I like Lili,
mistaking the puppets for the puppeteer,
not realizing that created things
are the means the Creator uses
to express love for me?

God is a giver.
And God has nothing to give but himself.
And to give himself is to do his deeds . . .
to be himself . . .
through the things he has made.

C. S. LEWIS

[Jesus said,] "When your eyes are sound, your whole body is full of light."

LUKE 11:34

Sunday newspapers used to carry a puzzle page. For example, one showed a picture of a family picnic. Beneath the picture was printed the question, "Can you find the girl hidden in this scene?" You would look and look but not see her. Then, suddenly, you would find her ear in a cloud, her mouth in a tree, and so on, until you would find the entire girl's smiling face. Once you found the girl, the picture was never the same again. It's like that in real life, also. There's a person hidden in every scene of our life. And that person is God. God is there as a giver of all that we are and of all that we have: life, talents, family, friends. Everything about us is God's gift of love to us.

When did I first begin to find the hidden God in the picture of my daily life?

To seek God, the greatest adventure;
to find God,
the greatest human achievement;
to fall in love with God,
the greatest of all romances.

RAPHAEL SIMON (slightly adapted)

The LORD who created you says,
"Do not be afraid—I will save you.
I have called you by name—you are mine."

ISAIAH 43:1

Marine Lieutenant Alan McLean stepped
on a mine in a rice paddy during a firefight
with the Vietcong. He said later, "I
remember sailing through the air and
hurting like hell." Both his legs were
blown off. Alan was evacuated by
helicopter. He said later, "I was close to
death on the chopper." Then something
unexplainable happened. "What came over
me," he said, "was the realization that
God loved me and you and all of us, that
God loved everyone in the world." This
thought was miraculously calming and
gave Alan a profound peace—a peace
unlike anything he had ever known, a
peace that has never left him.

How hard is it for me to find
the face of a loving God
in the problems and trials of my life?

Who never ate his bread in sorrow,
Who never spent the darksome hours,
Weeping and watching for the morrow,
He knows you not, you heavenly Power.

JOHANN WOLFGANG VON GOETHE

O God, you are my God,
and I long for you.
My whole being desires you;
like dry, worn-out, and waterless land,
my soul is thirsty for you.

PSALM 63:1

"Each time I visit my island off the coast
of Maine, I fall in love with the sea again.
Now I don't know all of the sea—wide
areas of it will always be unknown to
me—but I know the sea. It has a near
range. It washes my island. I can sit beside
it . . . and sail over it, and be sung to sleep
by the music of it. God is like that. [God]
is so great . . . that we can think of [God]
only in symbolic terms, but [God] has a
near range."

HARRY EMERSON FOSDICK

In what way, especially, do I experience
God's near range—how God "washes
my island" and sings love songs to me?
In what way, especially, do I experience
God's far range?

Songwriter Rod McKuen said,
"I love the sea, but that doesn't make me
less afraid of it." In a similar way,
Scripture speaks of a love and a fear
that we experience for God.

WEEK 35
Day 5

Whoever does not love
does not know God, for God is love.
And God showed [God's] love for us
by sending [God's] only Son into the world,
so that we might have life through him.

1 JOHN 4:8-9

An old priest told a young seminarian,
"Someday you will realize that God loves
you with an infinite love. When that
realization dawns on you, your life will
change for the better beyond anything you
dreamed possible." What the old priest
told the young seminarian is true of each
of us. God loves us with an infinite love.
That incredible truth is waiting to be born
in our hearts.

Why do I have difficulty realizing—
with my heart as well as my head—
that God loves me with a love beyond
anything I could imagine or dream?

God of love!
When the thought of you
awakens in my heart,
let it not be like a frightened bird,
thrashing about wildly,
but like a trusting child
waking from sleep with a smile.

SOREN KIERKEGAARD (free translation)

How good it is
to give thanks to you, O LORD,
to sing in your honor, O Most High God,
to proclaim your constant love
every morning
and your faithfulness every night. . . .
Because of what you have done,
I sing for joy.

PSALM 92:1-4

A college girl was making a retreat at
Saint Edward's University in Texas.
Suddenly she was moved deeply by God's
love for her. She wrote:
"What can I say as I live each day,
wanting to share myself with you? . . .
What can I say to you, my God,
but that I love you from the heart?
What can I say to you, my God?
All I can think is, 'Thank you, God!'
You have taught me how to live and pray.
You always care and won't lead me astray.
What can I say to you, my God?
All I can think is, 'Thank you, God!' "
LOURDES RUIZ ARTHUR

What can I say to you, my God?

O, Lord that lends me life,
Lend me a heart replete with thankfulness.
WILLIAM SHAKESPEARE

WEEK 35
Day 7 _____

*There is nothing in all creation
that will ever be able to separate us
from the love of God.*

ROMANS 8:39

A stanza from an old hymn describes
God's love in these poetic words:
"The love of God is greater far
Than tongue and pen can ever tell;
It goes beyond the highest star."
But the most moving stanza of the hymn
is the last one. James Montgomery Boice
says this stanza was not written by the
original composer, but was added later.
Found on the wall of a room in a mental
hospital, it reads:
"Could we with ink the ocean fill
And were the skies of parchment made;
Were every stalk on earth a quill,
And every man a scribe by trade;
To write the love of God above
Would drain the ocean dry;
Nor could the scroll contain the whole,
Though stretched from sky to sky."

How ready am I to give God the same place
in my heart that God has in the universe?

*Jesus Christ will be Lord of all,
or he will not be Lord at all.*

SAINT AUGUSTINE

WEEKLY MEETING
Sharing Agenda

1 To what extent do I tend to mistake the puppets for the puppeteer, the creatures for the Creator?

2 When did I begin to find the hidden God in the picture of my daily life?

3 How difficult is it for me to find the face of the loving God in the problems and trials of daily life? What problems, especially?

4 How do I experience the near range of God? The far range?

5 Why do I sometimes find it hard to realize—with my heart as well as my head—that God loves me beyond anything I could imagine?

6 What are some ways that I thank God for God's many gifts to me?

7 What keeps me from giving God the same place in my heart that God holds in the universe?

36 Take, Lord, and receive me!
(Contemplation: My Response)

An old story concerns a person who dove into a raging river and saved a drowning child. A few days later the child said to the person, "How can I ever thank you for what you did for me?" The person said, "The best thanks you can give me is to live the rest of your life in a way that will have made it worth saving."

What the person said to the child, God could say to each of us.

It is now up to us to thank God by living the rest of our lives in a way that will have made them worth saving.

This week's meditations focus on what response you can make to God for all that God has done for you. The grace you ask before each meditation is:

Lord, put into my heart
the love and the grace
to make this offering of myself to you:
Take, Lord,
and receive all my liberty, my memory,
my understanding, and my entire will—
all that I hold dear.

You have given all these things to me.
I now place them all at your service,
to be used as you wish.
Give me only your love and your grace.
These are enough for me.

Daily Reading

WEEK 36
Day 1

"Father! In your hands I place my spirit!"
LUKE 23:46

French philosopher Blaise Pascal had an
experience that changed his life. He
described it in these cryptic words:
"Monday, November 23, 1654,
from about 10:30 in the evening
until 12:30 at night: fire.
God of Abraham, God of Isaac,
God of Jacob, not the God
of the philosophers and scholars.
Certainty, joy, peace!
God of Jesus Christ!
He is only found along the ways
that are taught in the gospel.
Tears of joy!
I had parted from him.
Let me never again be separated
from him. Surrender to Jesus Christ!"

I beg God for the grace to pray joyfully,
"Take, Lord, and receive all my liberty."

We are all too much haunted by ourselves,
projecting the central shadow of self
on everything around us.
Then comes the Gospel to rescue us
from this selfishness.
Redemption is this, to forget self in God.
FREDERICK W. ROBERTSON

[Jesus] took a piece of bread,
gave thanks to God, broke it,
and gave it to them, saying,
"This is my body, which is given for you.
Do this in memory of me."

LUKE 22:19

In a *Science Digest* article entitled "The
Magic of Memory," Laurence Cherry says:
"Our memories are probably
our most cherished possessions.
More than anything else we own,
they belong uniquely to us,
defining our personalities and our views
of the world. Each of us can summon
thousands of memories at will:
our first day at school, a favorite
family pet, a summer house we loved."
Oscar Wilde had all this in mind
when he said, "Memory is the diary
that we all carry about with us."
And the German writer Jean Paul Richter
said, "Our memory is the only paradise
out of which we cannot be driven."

I beg God for the grace to pray joyfully,
"Take, Lord, and receive . . . my memory."

God gives us memory
so that we may have roses in December.

JAMES MATTHEW BARRIE

WEEK 36
Day 3

*In all things God works for good
with those who love [God].*

ROMANS 8:28

A student told a counselor, "Were it not
for this prayer card, I could not have
accepted my mother's death." It read:
"For ev'ry pain we must bear,
For ev'ry burden, ev'ry care,
There's a reason.
For ev'ry grief that bows the head,
For ev'ry teardrop that is shed,
There's a reason.
But if we trust God, as we should,
It will turn out for our good.
[God] knows the reason."
AUTHOR UNKNOWN

I beg God for the grace to pray joyfully,
"Take, Lord, and receive . . .
my understanding."

*"I will bless the person
who puts his trust in me.
He is like a tree growing near a stream
and sending out roots to the water.
It is not afraid when hot weather comes,
because its leaves stay green;
it has no worries when there is no rain;
it keeps on bearing fruit."*

JEREMIAH 17:7-8

[Jesus taught his disciples to pray,]
"Our Father . . . may your will be done."

MATTHEW 6:9-10

In 1911 Robert Scott and four British
explorers reached the South Pole after
traveling eight hundred miles on foot
through snow and bitter cold. On their
return trip, however, tragedy struck and
all five died. When their frozen bodies
were recovered, the last words that each
had written were still legible. Next to one
body was this brief note:
"So I live now,
knowing that I am in God's hands. . . .
We must do what we can
and leave the rest to [God]."

I beg God for the grace to pray joyfully,
"Take, Lord, and receive . . .
my entire will."

I just want to do God's will. . . .
[God's] allowed me to go to the mountain.
And I've looked over,
and I've seen the promised land. . . .
So I'm happy tonight.
I'm not worried about anything.
I'm not fearing any man.

MARTIN LUTHER KING, JR.
(the night before his death)

WEEK 36
Day 5

[Jesus gave us everything he had:
his love, his body, his blood, his life.
He had nothing more he could give.
So he cried out on the cross,] "Father!
In your hands I place my spirit!"

LUKE 23:46

Dr. Viktor Frankl was a prisoner of the
Nazis during World War II. In *Man's
Search for Meaning,* he writes about a side
of the camps we rarely hear of. He says:
"We who lived in concentration camps
can remember those who walked
through the huts comforting others,
giving away their last piece of bread.
They may have been few in number,
but they offer sufficient proof that
everything can be taken from a person
but one thing—the last freedom—to choose
one's attitude in any given set of
circumstances, to choose one's own way."

I beg God for the grace to pray joyfully,
"Take, Lord, and receive . . .
all that I hold dear."

Life is not a "brief candle."
It is a splendid torch that I want
to make burn as brightly
as possible for future generations.
GEORGE BERNARD SHAW

*[The Lord said,] "Whom shall I send? . . .
I answered, "I will go! Send me!"*

ISAIAH 6:8

Dag Hammarskjold became Secretary-
General of the United Nations in 1953.
He held that post until 1961, when he was
killed in a plane crash. When authorities
cleaned out his apartment, they found his
personal journal with a note attached to
it, saying that it could be published in
case of his death. One entry in the journal
concerned the turning point in his life.
It reads:
"I don't know
Who—or What—put the question.
I don't even know when it was put.
I don't even remember answering.
But at some moment I did answer yes
to Someone—or Something—and
at that hour I was certain existence
is meaningful and that, therefore,
my life in self-surrender had a goal."

I beg God for the grace to pray joyfully,
"Take, Lord, . . . all that I hold dear.
You have given all these things to me.
I now place them all at your service."

Man is too noble to serve anyone but God.
CARDINAL WYSZYNSKI

WEEK 36
Day 7 _____

*All I want is to know Christ and to
experience the power of his resurrection,
to share in his sufferings
and become like him in his death,
in the hope that I myself
will be raised from death to life.*

PHILIPPIANS 3:10-11

After his conversion to Christ, Japanese
social reformer Toyohiko Kagawa gave
up his comfortable home and went to live
in the slums of Kobe. There he shared
himself and his possessions with the
needy. In *Famous Life Decisions,* Cecil
Northcott says Kagawa gave away all his
clothing, keeping only a tattered kimono.
On one occasion, even though sick, he
preached to people in the rain, repeating
over and over, "God is love! God is love!
Where love is, there is God."

I beg God for the grace to pray joyfully,
"Take, Lord, . . .
all that I hold dear. . . .
Give me only your love and your grace.
These are enough for me."

*Our hearts were made for you,
O Lord, and they will not rest
until they rest in you.*

SAINT AUGUSTINE

WEEKLY MEETING
Sharing Agenda

1 When I think of surrendering to God all of my liberty—freedom to go where I want, do what I want, say what I want—what are some of the thoughts that enter my mind?

2 What is my earliest childhood memory? My fondest?

3 What is one thing in my life that I don't "understand" and would like to know God's reason for allowing it to happen? How easy is it for me to live totally by faith—not having to know the reason for things?

4 How joyfully and trustingly can I say to God, "Not my will, but thy will be done"—whatever it may be? Explain.

5 When I offer to God "all that I hold dear," what are some of the "dear" things I am talking about? Why would a loving God even want such things from me?

6 On a scale of one (minimally) to ten (totally), to what extent is my life being lived in total service to God?

7 How ready am I to hand God a blank check, saying, "Fill in any amount you want. Leave me only your love and your grace"?

Weekly Meeting Format

CALL TO PRAYER

Jesus said,
"I am the light of the world. . . .
Whoever follows me
will have the light of life
and will never walk in darkness."

JOHN 8:12

Lord Jesus, you also said
that where two or three
come together in your name,
you are there with them.
The light of this candle
symbolizes your presence among us.

And, Lord Jesus,
where you are,
there, too,
are the Father and the Holy Spirit.
So we begin our meeting
in the presence and the name
of the Father,
the Son,
and the Holy Spirit.